Violence
and Mental Health
Opportunities for Prevention and Early Detection

PROCEEDINGS OF A WORKSHOP

Deepali Patel, *Rapporteur*

Forum on Global Violence Prevention

Board on Global Health

Health and Medicine Division

The National Academies of
SCIENCES • ENGINEERING • MEDICINE

THE NATIONAL ACADEMIES PRESS
Washington, DC
www.nap.edu

THE NATIONAL ACADEMIES PRESS 500 Fifth Street, NW Washington, DC 20001

This project was supported by AB InBev; Administration for Community Living; Archstone; Avon Foundation; Becton, Dickinson and Company; Catholic Health Initiative; Department of Labor; Felix Foundation; JSI Research & Training Institute, Inc. (U.S. Agency for International Development); Kaiser Permanente; Leading Age; National Institute for the Evaluation of Education; National Institutes of Health; New Venture Fund; Oak Foundation; and Robert Wood Johnson Foundation. Any opinions, findings, conclusions, or recommendations expressed in this publication do not necessarily reflect the views of any organization or agency that provided support for the project.

International Standard Book Number-13: 978-0-309-46662-2
International Standard Book Number-10: 0-309-46662-8
Digital Object Identifier: https://doi.org/10.17226/24916

Additional copies of this publication are available for sale from the National Academies Press, 500 Fifth Street, NW, Keck 360, Washington, DC 20001; (800) 624-6242 or (202) 334-3313; http://www.nap.edu.

Copyright 2018 by the National Academy of Sciences. All rights reserved.

Printed in the United States of America

Suggested citation: National Academies of Sciences, Engineering, and Medicine. 2018. *Violence and mental health: Opportunities for prevention and early intervention: Proceedings of a workshop*. Washington, DC: The National Academies Press. doi: https://doi.org/10.17226/24916.

The National Academies of
SCIENCES • ENGINEERING • MEDICINE

The **National Academy of Sciences** was established in 1863 by an Act of Congress, signed by President Lincoln, as a private, nongovernmental institution to advise the nation on issues related to science and technology. Members are elected by their peers for outstanding contributions to research. Dr. Marcia McNutt is president.

The **National Academy of Engineering** was established in 1964 under the charter of the National Academy of Sciences to bring the practices of engineering to advising the nation. Members are elected by their peers for extraordinary contributions to engineering. Dr. C. D. Mote, Jr., is president.

The **National Academy of Medicine** (formerly the Institute of Medicine) was established in 1970 under the charter of the National Academy of Sciences to advise the nation on medical and health issues. Members are elected by their peers for distinguished contributions to medicine and health. Dr. Victor J. Dzau is president.

The three Academies work together as the **National Academies of Sciences, Engineering, and Medicine** to provide independent, objective analysis and advice to the nation and conduct other activities to solve complex problems and inform public policy decisions. The National Academies also encourage education and research, recognize outstanding contributions to knowledge, and increase public understanding in matters of science, engineering, and medicine.

Learn more about the National Academies of Sciences, Engineering, and Medicine at **www.nationalacademies.org**.

The National Academies of
SCIENCES • ENGINEERING • MEDICINE

Consensus Study Reports published by the National Academies of Sciences, Engineering, and Medicine document the evidence-based consensus on the study's statement of task by an authoring committee of experts. Reports typically include findings, conclusions, and recommendations based on information gathered by the committee and the committee's deliberations. Each report has been subjected to a rigorous and independent peer-review process and it represents the position of the National Academies on the statement of task.

Proceedings published by the National Academies of Sciences, Engineering, and Medicine chronicle the presentations and discussions at a workshop, symposium, or other event convened by the National Academies. The statements and opinions contained in proceedings are those of the participants and are not endorsed by other participants, the planning committee, or the National Academies.

For information about other products and activities of the National Academies, please visit www.nationalacademies.org/about/whatwedo.

PLANNING COMMITTEE ON MENTAL HEALTH AND VIOLENCE: OPPORTUNITES FOR PREVENTION AND EARLY INTERVENTION[1]

MARGARET M. MURRAY (*Co-Chair*), Director, Global Alcohol Research Program, National Institute on Alcohol Abuse and Alcoholism, National Institutes of Health
MARK L. ROSENBERG (*Co-Chair*), President and Chief Executive Officer, The Task Force for Global Health
ALBERT J. ALLEN, Senior Medical Fellow, Bioethics and Pediatric Capabilities, Global Medical Affairs and Development Center of Excellence, Eli Lilly and Company
MADELON BARANOSKI, Associate Professor of Psychiatry, Yale University School of Medicine
ROBERT BERNSTEIN, President and Executive Director, Judge David L. Bazelon Center for Mental Health and Law
JAMES BLAIR, Chief, Unit on Affective Cognitive Neuroscience, National Institute of Mental Health
C. HENDRICKS BROWN, Professor, Departments of Psychiatry and Behavioral Sciences and Preventive Medicine, Northwestern University Feinberg School of Medicine
ERIC CAINE, Co-Director, Center for the Study and Prevention of Suicide, University of Rochester
SHELDON GREENBERG, Professor, Division of Public Safety Leadership, Johns Hopkins University School of Education
VICKIE M. MAYS, Professor, Department of Health Policy and Management, University of California, Los Angeles

---

[1] The National Academies of Sciences, Engineering, and Medicine's planning committees are solely responsible for organizing the workshop, identifying topics, and choosing speakers. The responsibility for this published Proceedings of a Workshop rests with the workshop rapporteur and the institution.

FORUM ON GLOBAL VIOLENCE PREVENTION[1]

JACQUELYN C. CAMPBELL (*Co-Chair*), Anna D. Wolf Chair and Professor, Johns Hopkins University School of Nursing (Until December 2017)
MARK L. ROSENBERG (*Co-Chair*), President and Chief Executive Officer, The Task Force for Global Health (until March 2014)
ALBERT J. ALLEN, Senior Medical Fellow, Bioethics and Pediatric Capabilities, Global Medical Affairs and Development Center of Excellence, Eli Lilly and Company (until June 2014)
FRANCES ASHE-GOINS, Deputy Director, Office on Women's Health, U.S. Department of Health and Human Services (until August 2014)
SUSAN BISSELL, Associate Director, Child Protection Section, United Nations Children's Fund (until February 2014)
ARTURO CERVANTES TREJO, National Institute of Educational Evaluation, Mexico (until August 2017)
KATHY GREENLEE, Assistant Secretary for Aging, Administration on Aging, U.S. Department of Health and Human Services (until September 2016)
RODRIGO V. GUERRERO, Mayor, Cali, Colombia (until August 2017)
DAVID HEMENWAY, Professor of Health Policy; Director, Injury Control Research Center and the Youth Violence Prevention Center, Harvard University School of Public Health (until December 2014)
FRANCES HENRY, Advisor, F Felix Foundation (until June 2016)
L. ROWELL HUESMANN, Amos N. Tversky Collegiate Professor of Psychology and Communication Studies; Director, Research Center for Group Dynamics, Institute for Social Research, University of Michigan (until June 2014)
CAROL M. KURZIG, President, Avon Foundation for Women (until September 2014)
VALERIE MAHOLMES, Chief, Pediatric Trauma and Critical Illness Branch, National Institutes of Health (until September 2015)
BRIGID McCAW, Medical Director, NCal Family Violence Prevention Program, Kaiser Permanente (until August 2017)
JAMES A. MERCY, Special Advisor for Strategic Directions, Division of Violence Prevention, National Center for Injury Prevention and Control, Centers for Disease Control and Prevention (until August 2017)

---

[1] The National Academies of Sciences, Engineering, and Medicine's forums and roundtables do not issue, review, or approve individual documents. The responsibility for this published Proceedings of a Workshop rests with the workshop rapporteur and the institution.

MICHELE MOLONEY-KITTS, Managing Director, Together for Girls (until December 2016)
LAURA MOSQUEDA, Associate Dean of Primary Care, University of California, Irvine, School of Medicine (until August 2017)
MARGARET M. MURRAY, Director, Global Alcohol Research Program, National Institute on Alcohol Abuse and Alcoholism, National Institutes of Health (until September 2015)
JOHN T. PICARELLI, Program Manager for Transnational Issues, National Institute of Justice
COLLEEN SCANLON, Senior Vice President, Advocacy, Catholic Health Initiatives (until August 2017)
MAISHA SIMMONS, Program Officer, Vulnerable Populations Team, Robert Wood Johnson Foundation (until May 2016)
EVELYN TOMASZEWSKI, Senior Policy Advisor, Human Rights and International Affairs, National Association of Social Workers (until August 2017)
ELIZABETH WARD, Chair, Violence Prevention Alliance, University of the West Indies, Mona Campus (until August 2017)

Health and Medicine Division Staff

AUDREY GROCE, Senior Program Assistant (until September 2014)
RACHEL M. TAYLOR, Associate Program Officer (until August 2014)
KIMBERLY SCOTT, Senior Program Officer (until May 2015)
KATHERINE BLAKESLEE, Global Program Advisor, Board on Global Health (until December 2014)
JULIE PAVLIN, Senior Board Director (from November 2016)
KATHERINE PEREZ, Senior Program Assistant (from August 2017)
JULIE WILTSHIRE, Financial Associate (until November 2014)
PATRICK W. KELLEY, Senior Board Director, Board on Global Health (until July 2016)

Reviewers

This Proceedings of a Workshop was reviewed in draft form by individuals chosen for their diverse perspectives and technical expertise. The purpose of this independent review is to provide candid and critical comments that will assist the National Academies of Sciences, Engineering, and Medicine in making each published proceedings as sound as possible and to ensure that it meets the institutional standards for quality, objectivity, evidence, and responsiveness to the charge. The review comments and draft manuscript remain confidential to protect the integrity of the process.

We thank the following individuals for their review of this proceedings:

ALBERT J. ALLEN, Eli Lilly and Company
MEDELON V. BARANOSKI, Yale School of Medicine
GREG BROWN, Nipissing University
PAOLO DEL VECCHIO, Substance Abuse and Mental Health Services Administration

Although the reviewers listed above provided many constructive comments and suggestions, they were not asked to endorse the content of the proceedings nor did they see the final draft before its release. The review of this proceedings was overseen by **NANCY E. ADLER**, University of California, San Francisco. She was responsible for making certain that an independent examination of this proceedings was carried out in accordance with standards of the National Academies and that all review comments were carefully considered. Responsibility for the final content rests entirely with the rapporteur and the National Academies.

Contents

1 **OVERVIEW** 1
Forum on Global Violence Prevention, 1
Workshop Objectives, 2
Organization of the Proceedings of a Workshop, 3

2 **FRAMING THE PARADIGM** 5
Violence and Mental Illness: What Do We Know?
  What Do We Need? What Can We Do?, 5
Operational Definitions for the Workshop, 8
Ecological Framework, 10
Relationship Between Mental Illness and Violence, 15
Neurocognitive Mechanisms of Violent Behavior, 17
References, 19

3 **AT THE INTERSECTION OF MENTAL HEALTH AND** 21
  VIOLENCE
Experiences and Perspectives Related to Mental Health and
  Violence, 21
Detecting and Assessing Mental Health Dysfunction and Risk
  for Violence, 26
References, 33

| 4 | **MEANS AND MODIFIERS** | 35 |

Restricting the Means of Violence, 35
Alcohol, Alcohol Use Disorders, and Violence, 41
References, 48

| 5 | **PREVENTION, INTERVENTION, AND TREATMENT** | 51 |

Mental Health Services and Violence, 51
Interface with the Justice Community and Opportunities for
  Intervention, 56
References, 65

| 6 | **ASSEMBLING THE PIECES AND INTEGRATING ELEMENTS** | 67 |

Evaluation of Programs for Violence Prevention and
  Mental Health Promotion, 67
Reflections and the Way Forward, 69
References, 74

APPENDIXES
A Workshop-Related Discussion Papers 75
B Workshop Agenda 129
C Workshop Speaker Biographies 139

Boxes, Figures, and Tables

BOXES

1-1 Statement of Task, 3

5-1 Issues Across the Criminal Justice System, 58
5-2 What Police Patrol Officers Want Mental Health Practitioners to Know, 59

FIGURES

A-1 Mental health expenditures, 101
A-2 The impact of being bullied on functioning in adulthood, 121
A-3 Adjusted mean young adult CRP levels (mg/L) based on childhood/adolescent bullying status, 123

TABLES

A-1 Mental Health Professionals in LAC, 102
A-2 Number of Users Attending Mental Health Facilities, 103

1

Overview[1]

On February 26–27, 2014, the National Academies of Sciences, Engineering, and Medicine's Forum on Global Violence Prevention convened a workshop titled Mental Health and Violence: Opportunities for Prevention and Early Intervention. The workshop brought together advocates and experts in public health and mental health, anthropology, biomedical science, criminal justice, global health and development, and neuroscience to examine experience, evidence, and practice at the intersection of mental health and violence. Participants explored how violence impacts mental health and how mental health influences violence and discussed approaches to improve research and practice in both domains.

FORUM ON GLOBAL VIOLENCE PREVENTION

This workshop was the seventh in a series of workshops held by the Forum on Global Violence Prevention, which works to promote research on both protective and risk factors, to encourage evidence-based prevention efforts, and to facilitate dialogue and exchange by bringing together experts from all areas of violence prevention. The forum is tasked as follows:

---

[1] The planning committee's role was limited to planning the workshop. The Proceedings of a Workshop was prepared by the rapporteur as a factual account of what occurred at the workshop. Statements, recommendations, and opinions expressed are those of individual presenters and participants and are not necessarily endorsed or verified by the National Academies of Sciences, Engineering, and Medicine. They should not be construed as reflecting any group consensus.

- Provides an ongoing, regular, evidence-based, impartial setting for the multidisciplinary exchange of information and ideas concerning violence prevention
- Illuminates policy, research, and practice priorities worthy of further study or investment
- Gathers information on the scientific basis and public health needs pertinent to global violence prevention

Past workshops have explored the evidentiary basis of violence prevention, the contagion of violence, the social and economic costs of violence, and violence against women and children, among other topics.

WORKSHOP OBJECTIVES

In her introductory comments, planning committee co-chair Peggy Murray of the National Institute on Alcohol Abuse and Alcoholism explained that this workshop on mental health and violence prevention emerged from discussions held during previous workshops, as well as current events and media reports. She noted that what is known about mental health and violence prevention is complicated, and what is not known is vast. Law enforcement officials, in particular, are burdened by the number of people with mental illness they encounter and are not well equipped to deal with these numbers outside of traditional corrective means. Planning committee co-chair Mark Rosenberg of The Task Force for Global Health further explained that the intersection of mental health and violence is confusing. Is the relationship unidirectional, and in which way, or is it bidirectional? The workshop planning committee sought to shed light on this issue to gain a clearer picture of this interaction.

Because the relationship between mental health and violence is complex, complicated, and of interest to numerous stakeholders, the planning committee acknowledged that it was not feasible to conduct an exhaustive review in a 2-day workshop (see Box 1-1 for the Statement of Task). Thus, the committee identified the following topics as important to address:

- A description of mental health function as a continuum, from optimal to dysfunctional, with problems ranging from minor to serious distress to antisocial behavior to severe mental illness
- Perpetration of violence, victims of violence, and exposure to violence
- Interpersonal, self-directed, and collective violence
- Neurobiology of violent behavior
- Multiple ecological levels to be considered
- A life-course/developmental perspective

> **BOX 1-1**
> **Statement of Task**
>
> An ad hoc committee will plan a 2-day public workshop to explore the relationship between mental health and violence. The workshop will feature invited presentations and discussions with the goal of laying the foundation for progress in improving outcomes with respect to mental health and violence embodied in research, policy change, and program development.
>
> Workshop speakers and participants will explore a continuum of approaches to improving both mental health and violence prevention with these objectives:
>
> - Arriving at a better understanding of the intersection of mental health and violence, including
>   - the relationship between mental health dysfunction and risks of violence perpetration and victimization, as well as the mental health consequences of exposure to violence; and
>   - the extent to which improved mental health functioning and improved mental health services can—or cannot—address concerns about violence in society.
> - Exploring a new model for thinking about the intersection of mental health promotion and violence prevention that is useful for improving outcomes

- Means of violence perpetration, including access to weapons
- Identification of the multiple sectors that must be involved, as well as their intersection

ORGANIZATION OF THE PROCEEDINGS OF A WORKSHOP

This Proceedings of a Workshop provides a summary account of the workshop presentations and the expert papers submitted by workshop speakers. This proceedings comprises six chapters, including this introduction. Chapter 2, Framing the Paradigm, presents opening remarks from the keynote speaker, Thomas Insel; operational definitions from Vickie Mays; an ecological framework approach from Eric Caine and Janis Jenkins; an exploration of the intersection of mental illness and violence from Mark Rosenberg (speaking on behalf of Paul Applebaum); and the neurobiology of violent behavior from Jim Blair. Chapter 3, At the Intersection of Mental Health and Violence, details lived experiences and perspectives on mental health and violence, as presented by Daniel Fisher, Elyn Saks, Harvey Rosenthal, and Robert Bernstein. The chapter also outlines information on assessing and detecting mental health dysfunction and risk of violence from the presentations of Seena Fazel, Dustin Pardini, and Dieter Wolke.

Chapter 4, Means and Modifiers, includes presentations on restricting the means of violence from Daniel Webster, Michael Phillips, and Mike Luo; and on alcohol and alcohol use disorders from Klaus Miczek, Kenneth Leonard, Toben Nelson, and Ronaldo Laranjeira. Chapter 5, Prevention, Intervention, and Treatment, covers mental health services and violence from Colleen Barry, Sharon Stephan, and Dévora Kestel, and the interface with the justice community from Madelon Baronski, Sheldon Greenberg, Ray Kotwicki, David Wexler, and Patrick Fox. The final chapter, Assembling the Pieces and Integrating Elements, includes a presentation on an evaluation of interventions by Hendricks Brown, and a synthesis of the summary panel and subsequent discussion on the way forward.

2

Framing the Paradigm

The opening panels of the workshop set the stage for the subsequent discussions. The keynote address provided an overview of the evidence for and the policy involving mental illness and its relationship to violence. Speakers presented on operational definitions, ecological frameworks, cultural context, risk and protective factors, and neurobiology. They noted the common misperception that mental illness plays a greater role in the risk of violence than it actually does. Although, under certain circumstances, persons with mental illness are indeed at a greater risk of violence to others and, in general, are at greater risk for suicide.

VIOLENCE AND MENTAL ILLNESS: WHAT DO WE KNOW? WHAT DO WE NEED? WHAT CAN WE DO?[1]

Mental health and violence are often addressed in a manner that adds to the confusion rather than the clarity, stated Tom Insel in his keynote address, and it is important to disseminate accurate and evidence-based information about the relationship between the two. Currently, he remarked, there is tremendous focus from the public on mass violence (e.g., shootings) and linking it to mental illness—a situation that requires untangling. Insel evoked President Barack Obama's suggested action plan to address gun violence and mental health services, noting that these issues go beyond the

---

[1] This section summarizes information presented by Tom Insel, National Institute of Mental Health.

domain of criminal justice and point to social inequities. Public health tools are essential in reducing violence, Insel asserted.

At the highest levels of the U.S. government, there is both a desire to address the recent shootings in schools and public places and a hesitancy to directly address gun violence. This desire has translated into transforming mental health care to reduce additional violence. Furthermore, Insel remarked that the framing of mental health and violence on the same axis—though done with good intentions—has resulted in more misconceptions. To highlight this point, he shared the following data:

- Untreated active psychosis, whether because of mental illness or drug use, is associated with irrational behavior, which could include violence. Notably, 38 to 48 percent of the homicides and suicides associated with people who are diagnosed with schizophrenia or bipolar disorder occur at the beginning of illness, often before treatment and sometimes before a diagnosis (Nielssen et al., 2012; Short et al., 2013). That risk of violence is most likely to be directed toward family and friends.
- People with treated mental illness are at no higher risk for committing violence than the general population and are at higher risk for being the victims of violence. Scandinavian studies have indicated that treatment of mental illness can reduce violence risk 15-fold (Nielssen and Large, 2010).
- Violence associated with a diagnosed serious mental illness is more likely to be self-directed than directed at others, even if one includes family and friends. Ninety percent of the approximately 38,000 suicides each year in the United States involve mental illness, while less than 5 percent of the approximately 14,000 homicides each year involve mental illness (CDC, 2005). Insel calculated this to be a 50-fold differential. Occasionally, as was the case in the school shooting in Newtown, Connecticut, an event might include homicide before suicide.
- The risk of suicide is greater in people with mental illness than in the general population—almost half to three-quarters of the population-wide suicide risk can be explained by mental illness (Hawton and Heeringen, 2009). The lifetime risk of suicide for men with mental illness is 4.3 percent, and for women, it is 2.1 percent, whereas it is 0.7 percent and 0.2 percent for men and women without mental illness, respectively.
- Misinformation exists around a supposed increase in homicides in the United States when in fact it has decreased from 9.8 per 100,000 people in 1990 to 4.8 per 100,000 in 2010. On the other hand, suicide rates have remained relatively stable over the past

20 years. Other causes of mortality, including road traffic fatalities, have also dropped in that same time frame.
- The United States is disproportionately represented in firearm deaths among high-income countries, accounting for almost 80 percent of the total. For people 15 to 24 years old (i.e., the peak period for developing psychotic illness), the risk of homicide involving a firearm is 42 times higher and suicide involving a firearm is 8.8 times higher, relative to other countries (Richardson and Hemenway, 2011).

Insel referenced the popular perception that although the number of homicides has decreased, mass shootings have increased. He questioned this conclusion, as these are relatively rare events; while there is potential for this trend, the evidence is not clear. These tragic events capture national attention even though they are a small part of overall risk.

Because violence is a relatively rare event (even if it does not seem rare), it is difficult to predict at the individual level which prevention efforts will be the most effective. From a public health perspective, means restriction can work to reduce both homicide and suicide, he asserted. The knowledge on how to do so exists but can be a difficult sell in the policy arena. To this end, Insel emphasized that to the extent that mental illness is a risk factor for violence, treatment can help reduce it.

Treatment, however, is usually targeted to specific populations. Insel described the findings of a mapping exercise used to determine the domains in which suicides occur. Some populations, such as military personnel, do not constitute a large proportion of the overall group of suicides. Others, such as emergency department workers and health care providers, are a much larger percentage. Deaths from gun violence compose the largest portion. To reduce suicides, Insel proposed four measures for continued exploration, refinement, and improvement:

1. Predictors of risk and resilience, though he acknowledged this would be a difficult path
2. Surveillance, as data on suicides lag by almost 3 years
3. Tools for prevention and treatment
4. Evidenced-based policies for limiting access to means

An important measure that could be undertaken now is to better assist adolescents who are on the pathway to psychosis. In the United States, the duration of untreated psychosis is about 110 weeks—more than 2 years. One program the National Institute of Mental Health (NIMH) supports to address this issue is called RAISE (Recovery After an Initial Schizophrenia Episode), which ensures that following a diagnosis, a person receives a package of treatment in a family-centered approach with a goal of improving function in addition to reducing symptoms. This program is currently being implemented in a few states, with data collection efforts under way to determine its effectiveness.

A second measure Insel recommended is to move upstream in terms of interventions. Early detection and early intervention have reduced mortality in other areas and have the potential to reduce violence, as well. Rather than focusing on the "21-year-old who's been psychotic for 2 years and now gets a label in a treatment program, [focus should be placed on] the 15-year-old who's at highest risk, and figuring out what could be provided to that 15-year-old so that at 19 he or she doesn't have a psychotic illness," Insel explained. He expressed that treatment is not only medication, but a whole series of interventions that build resilience and executive function, provide family psychoeducation and peer support, and improve other skills.

Insel closed with a few summary remarks:

- Most people with mental illness are not violent, and most acts of violence are not committed by people with mental illness.
- Some people with mental illness are a danger to themselves and others.
- Fear of those with mental illness confounds the assessment of risk (i.e., people with mental illness are more likely to be victims than perpetrators).
- Early detection and early treatment can reduce risk.

In the question-and-answer session following Insel's presentation, additional salient points were raised. In terms of means restriction, participants discussed that the people who attempt suicide are often somewhat ambivalent about their success—restricting one's means does not often result in the substitution of another means. Additionally, Insel emphasized that school-based interventions should not be focused on addressing mental illness, which often has not developed by adolescence, but rather on reframing the issue as improving adolescents' school performance and relationship skills. The majority of those who demonstrate "precursors" do not develop mental illness, he noted.

OPERATIONAL DEFINITIONS FOR THE WORKSHOP[2]

Several workshop participants and speakers mentioned that confusion and miscommunication abound in the field of mental health, in no small

---

[2] This section summarizes information presented by Vickie Mays, University of California, Los Angeles.

part due to the ambiguity around terms. Vickie Mays noted that even the term "mental health" is confusing; some equate it with mental illness, while others place it on the side of well-being. To create a foundation for workshop discussions, Mays presented a series of operational definitions for common terminology in the field.

Mental health is defined as "a state of well-being in which the individual realizes his or her own abilities, can cope with the normal stresses of life, can work productively and fruitfully, and is able to make a contribution to his or her community" (WHO, 2001).

On **mental illness,** Mays acknowledged there is no one encompassing definition because perspectives, such as health care assessment and justice, often have different aims. However, despite this difficulty, stakeholders share a common goal of developing research that produces better predictors, interventions, and treatments.

On the other hand, **severe mental illness (SMI)** has a greater consensus in definition and comprises several disorders including bipolar disorder, depression, obsessive compulsive disorder (OCD), panic disorder, post-traumatic stress disorder (PTSD), and schizophrenia. SMI is disruptive, not only for individuals, but also for families, communities, and sometimes in the broader system. On the positive side, there are treatments, including not just medication but also therapies. One important policy direction is ensuring these treatments reach the people who need them. "In terms of serious mental illness, we need to remember that recovery is possible when we can get these treatments to people in an effective manner and in a timely manner," she stated.

The *Diagnostic and Statistical Manual of Mental Disorders, Fifth Edition* (DSM-5), defines a **mental disorder** as "a syndrome characterized by clinically significant disturbance in an individual's cognition, emotion regulation, or behavior that reflects a dysfunction in the psychological, biological, or developmental processes underlying mental functioning" (APA, 2013). While Mays acknowledges some level of controversy around the DSM-5 system, she highlighted the key elements of the definition of a syndrome that is characterized by "clinically significant disturbance" in the areas of cognition, emotional regulation, and behavior (APA, 2013).

Violence, as defined by the World Health Organization (WHO), is the "intentional use of physical force or power, threatened or actual, against oneself, another person, or against a group or community, that either results in or has a high likelihood of resulting in injury, death, psychological harm, maldevelopment, or deprivation" (WHO, 1996). Mays emphasized the broad definition in thinking about interventions.

Conduct disorder refers to a group of behavioral and emotional problems that usually begin during childhood or teenage years. Children with the disorder have "long-term, continual patterns of behavior" that tend to impact others or go against what is deemed typical by society for their age group (WHO, 1996). Mays explained that this particular concept was important because of the age of occurrence and because it is associated with more severe behavior later in life. She cautioned that some symptoms of conduct behavior, such as rule breaking, are also indicative of other disorders such as attention deficit hyperactivity disorder (ADHD) or abuse victimization, and that physical, family, school, and social factors could also explain the behavior. Moreover, several factors could contribute to the development of conduct disorder, including brain damage, child abuse, genetic vulnerability, school failure, and traumatic life experiences.

Alcohol use disorder is a pattern of consumption that results in clinically significant impairment or distress with a cluster of behavioral or physical symptoms, which can include withdrawal, craving, and tolerance. In the DSM-5, alcohol use disorder can be mild, moderate, or severe (APA, 2013).

Similarly, **substance use disorder** is marked by a constellation of cognitive, behavioral, and physiological symptoms and a continued use of a substance despite the harm it causes.

Perpetrator refers to the person who has actually committed the violent act or is responsible for it occurring. However, Mays stated that sometimes perpetrators have been or are currently victims themselves. Additionally, perpetrators are often addressed within the legal context, which only defines the person by his or her action at the time and does not address either the likelihood of reoccurrence or the measures that might prevent reoccurrence.

Victim refers to the person who has been "directly and proximately harmed as a result of the commission of an offense for which restitution may be ordered" (USSC, 2011). This is a legal definition, Mays noted. In terms of victims, stakeholders should examine the range of interventions needed to make a person whole and functional again.

Participants further discussed these definitions, noting that the variety of stakeholders with their different perspectives also have varying definitions. As science in the field advances and the biological basis of mental illness is further illuminated, these definitions can be refined. Depending on the aims and the principles of a particular discipline, however, definitions can be narrowed or expanded. Mays explained that these definitions are evolving in the context of a changing health care field, in which both services and actors are continuously being defined.

ECOLOGICAL FRAMEWORK

The ecological framework session included an overview and discussions of risk and protective factors and intervention points related to mental health and violence at the individual, relationship, community, and societal levels.

Models for Suicide Prevention and Treatment[3]

The focus of the workshop spans a range of problems that "encompass individuals' unique life circumstances, communities, societies, and the globe all into one thoughtful discussion," Eric Caine observed. This is chaotic, he noted, but holds possibility for intervention. On a national level, it is possible to prevent suicide. Notably, homicides and road traffic fatalities have decreased in part because of interventions when the outcomes were predictable at the population level, if not at the individual level. Although violence prevention has traditionally fallen under the purview of the criminal justice system, the responses have usually been reactionary. In the case of suicide, Caine explained, a reactionary response is one that is too late. He also observed that violence has a major global dimension: suicide, self-harm, interpersonal violence, war, and conflict are all very different around the world. However, looking at the burden of disease, suicide far outweighs the combined international impact of war and interpersonal violence.

In the United States, suicides not only carry a larger burden than homicides, but they are also substantially underestimated, particularly self-poisoning. Deliberate self-poisoning is not the same as unintentional poisoning, but occasionally "unintentional" means unable to determine intent and not specifically accidental. When the number of suicides is combined with the number of self-poisonings of uncertain intent, fatalities due to self-injury climb to approximately 50,000 per year. Caine also stated that firearms account for half of suicides, mostly due to their lethality (CDC, 2005). Because most people who attempt suicide and fail do not make another attempt, restricting lethal means could potentially reduce suicides, he argued.

The increase in suicides over the past decade has mostly been seen in the middle years of life in both men and women—not in youth. While the bulk of prevention resources is directed at youth, the suicide rate is highest among middle-aged white men, who compose a relatively small part of the population. The middle years are the most common time for women to commit suicide, as well. Caine further noted that suicides are not equally distributed across the United States. In ways not yet fully understood, suicide is driven by community and by location. In fact, suicides by poisoning and by firearm overlap significantly. There is also geographical variation in the suicide rate: it is higher in rural areas than in urban areas, whereas the opposite is true of homicides.

Across the United States, there is no uniform picture of self-directed violence or interpersonal violence. However, there are common

---

[3] This section summarizes information presented by Eric Caine, University of Rochester Medical Center.

community-level factors that may lead to violent injuries. He noted that, although people often choose to focus on one type of violence or another, prevention should be addressed earlier in the trajectory.

Caine shared an ecological model from WHO, which explores the overlap among different levels in determining risk and protective factors of violence. There are risks at the individual, interpersonal, community, and societal levels, all of which offer potential points of intervention. In fact, some interventions occur at multiple levels or require cooperation with other interventions, such as youth and family prevention programs. Caine cautioned that exploring all levels and factors at one time can be overwhelming.

Risk is a cumulative "unfolding phenomenon," he explained. All risks do not happen at once. This yields several points of potential intervention along a developmental pathway. He shared a model that depicted risks as a mountain range: the peaks are violent outcomes; the bases are larger social, economic, and family factors; and in the middle are individual and situational factors. In terms of interventions, the base includes those that are universal, while clinical ones are at the top; in the middle are selected and indicated interventions. Addressing the bottom and the middle would be necessary to make a difference, he stated.

Insel shared a second framework developed from the Haddon Matrix, which examines injury through the lens of multiple layers (i.e., individual, agent, and environment) and along a continuum of the event (i.e., pre-event, during, and post-event). This model, adapted for suicide, provides a starting point for the integration of neurobiological research and social research, as well as policy analysis.

He closed by sharing a third model focused on treatment, called the health impact pyramid. The pyramid shows that selected clinical interventions sit at the top and have a smaller population-level impact. Interventions at the bottom of the pyramid, which are more universal, have a greater population-level impact.

Culture, Mental Health, and Violence[4]

Cultural meaning is essential in considering the intersection of mental health and violence, and what it means for a person to accept treatment or medication, explained Janis Jenkins. A cultural lens highlights multiple perspectives and subjective experiences in a global, comparative context. From her research, which is team based and employs mixed methods including clinical diagnostic criteria, statistical analysis, and ethnography,

---

[4] This section summarizes information presented by Janis Jenkins, University of California, San Diego.

she observed that culture overlaps sectors of the ecological framework and is central to mental health and illness. She described several fundamental aspects of mental illness that are shaped by culture:

- Risk and vulnerability factors (e.g., gender inequity)
- Symptom content, form, and constellation
- Clinical diagnostic process
- Illness experience: identification, explanatory model, and meaning
- Kin emotional response and bonds and attachment
- Community social support stigma
- Service use and preferred treatment modalities
- Resources for resilience and recovery
- Course and outcome

In terms of symptoms, Jenkins advised further attention to not only whether the symptom is present, but how it presents, as well as how symptoms aggregate. Furthermore, culture influences what is considered typical and atypical, how explanatory models are developed, how those with mental illness are viewed, how the illness course proceeds, and what outcomes develop. She further explained that whether mental illness is perceived as a personality defect or a legitimate illness affects the experience of illness as well as the recovery.

What is involved in culture and conceptualizing it? She noted that perception of the self is highly variable. In some places, the self is more individualistic or self-centered, while in others the self is more socio-centric. This orientation of the self influences assumptions about the world and one's place in it, particularly in terms of labeling or self-identification. Emotions are also products of cultural systems and cultural rules.

In a cross-cultural survey of four African societies, perceptions of psychosis were examined (Edgerton, 1966). When queried on the behaviors associated with psychosis, participants responded in a similar manner: they were not tolerant of, and were concerned about, murder, assault, and disruptive behaviors. "These data show both a kind of universality to the conceptions of psychosis as well as some cultural specificity," she stated.

In terms of violence, Jenkins shared ways in which culture can broaden the understanding of violence. Many developing countries have high rates of homicide, particularly Belize, Côte d'Ivoire, El Salvador, Guatemala, Honduras, Jamaica, Malawi, and Zambia; and among developed countries, the United States outstrips its peers. Violence is not uniform; rather, cultural, socioeconomic, and political factors influence violence and instability in these arenas can particularly disadvantage individuals with increased vulnerability to violence. Subjective dimensions and structural arrangements of violence, she postulated, could offer greater insight. These would include conceptualizing violence as ordinary, contextually specific, lived experience, or an organized set of ideologies and practice. Structural violence, exerted systematically, causes harm or violence and disadvantages groups of people (Farmer, 2004). Examples include ethnocentrism, poverty, racism, and sexism, all of which constrain individual agency.

Jenkins further described research she had undertaken, investigating "the nexus among the role of the state in constructing a political ethos, the personal emotions of those who dwell in that ethos, and the mental health consequences for refugees or displaced persons" (Jenkins, 1991). Researchers have examined the experience of refugees fleeing political violence and identified terms to describe that experience, including "calor" or an intense feeling of heat that was presenting in the emergency room. They found in their study population that people had symptoms of PTSD and depression, but were also working hard to raise money to send home to their families. This raised the concept of "engaged depression" and the importance of resilience. She and her colleagues proposed that "calor" was a cultural manifestation of the political ethos of fear and violence inflicted by the state, presenting in a physical aspect. They used this concept to understand the connection among "symptom, emotion, culture, bodily experience, [and] political ethos."

In her concluding remarks, Jenkins described research into youth violence and mental health issues, showing links with structural issues such as poverty. She also noted a lack of gender difference in both perpetration and victimization. The ethnographic analysis also suggested that youth who are preoccupied with issues of violence have comorbid mental health conditions, as well.

Discussion

Following the presentations, speakers delved into the concepts and themes they raised. They spoke of the failure of detecting mental illness related to violence before the occurrence of such violence, particularly suicide. Caine remarked that instead of focusing on individual risk, going "upstream" at the population level means examining life circumstances in the community and the family. The need to address the "bottom of the pyramid" is felt around the world, and there is "tremendous commonality around community engagement," he continued. However, the focus is too often on suicide or homicide as an individual problem, partly because of the stigma around mental health. Caine also emphasized the importance of assessing the continuum of the problem rather than the event itself, which would include considering morbidity and disability when assessing the burden of violence, and not just at mortality. Jenkins added that addressing these societal issues would mean rethinking the concept of resource scarcity and instead generating political will to build the needed capacity.

RELATIONSHIP BETWEEN MENTAL ILLNESS AND VIOLENCE[5]

Mark Rosenberg presented information prepared by Paul Appelbaum on the evidence base for the relationship between mental illness and violence. Rosenberg began with the four conclusions of the presentation:

- The public perceives a strong relationship between mental health and violence.
- Although the rates of violence are increased in patients with serious mental illness, the relative risk is moderate and well below those public popular perceptions.
- Mental illness accounts for only a small proportion of the overall violence risk.
- Beyond substance abuse, it is the case that hostility, suspiciousness, agitation, and psychotic experiences may further increase the risk of violent behavior; however, violence is varied and multicausal, which has implications for both prediction and treatment.

Rosenberg addressed definitional issues around the concept of risk, including perceived risk, measured risk, absolute risk versus relative risk, and population-attributable risk. The intersection of mental health and violence is highly dependent on how these terms are defined. Additionally, he asked, what is the mechanism for increased risk? Mental health includes not only the biological basis of mental illness, but also the orientation of the individual within the family, society, and greater cultural context. Violence can be defined as physical, psychological, or emotional, Rosenberg explained, and it can result in death or injury, both physical and psychological. Threat could also be considered a form of violence.

The definition of mental illness is inconsistent in the literature. Some studies look at schizophrenia only, and others look at serious mental illnesses. Some look at Axis I disorders, while others look at personality disorders, or a combination of the two. Substance use disorders can be included as well. Because of this lack of agreement, comparative analyses should be performed carefully to ensure comparisons are equal. Appelbaum's intention was to focus on studies that examine violence toward others and their relationship with Axis I disorders and substance abuse, because methods and definitions are more refined in this area.

---

[5] This section summarizes information presented by Mark Rosenberg, Task Force for Global Health, with information prepared by Paul Appelbaum, Columbia University.

In looking at the perceived risk of violence by people with mental illness, Rosenberg noted that the public sees a strong relationship. The General Social Survey (GSS) provides some illustrative data. For the GSS, people were queried about the risk of violence in a specific situation. The situation involved a hypothetical person named John whose mental health is described as deteriorating over a period of a few months, until he became housebound, neglected his hygiene, and began to hear voices. Participants in the survey responded that if John had schizophrenia, it was 61 percent likely that he would commit violence; if major depression, then 34 percent; and if drug dependence, then 87 percent. Rosenberg also cited a public opinion survey in which 46 percent of participants thought people with a serious mental illness are "by far more dangerous" than the general population; and one-third thought locating a group home for people with mental illness in a residential neighborhood endangered local residents (Smith et al., 2013).

Though these data indicate that perceived risk is vastly exaggerated, evidence does suggest that there is an incremental risk associated with mental illness. The Epidemiologic Catchment Area Surveys looked at violence in the year prior in a sample representative of the general population. Researchers defined violence as hitting or throwing things at a partner or spouse, hitting a child and causing injury, using a weapon in a fight, and fighting while drinking. They looked at the distribution of violent risk and found that the percentage of violent people in the group with no diagnosed disorder was 2 percent. By specific diagnostic groups, there was an increasingly elevated risk of violent behavior: 2.37 percent in those with anxiety disorders, 8.36 percent in those with schizophrenia, and up to 21.3 percent in those with substance use disorder (NIMH, 1991).

Rosenberg stated that Appelbaum examined a second dataset, the National Epidemiologic Survey on Alcohol and Related Conditions, which assessed violence in the past year and mental illness. For those with mental illness, the relative risk of violence was 2.0, serious mental illness was 3.5, and substance use disorder was 3.3; for serious mental illness plus substance use disorder, it was 11.5 (NIAAA, 2005). Notably, the highest risk was found with the combination of mental illness and substance use disorder. At the same time, Appelbaum cautions that relative risk is dependent on the comparison group, and the general population might not be the best control.

In another study, the MacArthur Violence Risk Assessment Study, 1,000 people were followed for 1 year after discharge and interviewed every 10 weeks. They were compared with people in their own neighborhoods. In the first 10 weeks after discharge, people with mental illness did have an elevated risk compared with the community, which was higher when substance use disorders were included. Additionally, when using the appropriate control groups, the relative risk of violence for discharged individuals within the study community decreased slightly compared with results of relative risk in the general population. When controlling for substance abuse, this relative risk almost disappeared. It is the combination of substance abuse and mental illness that saw the highest increase.

Rosenberg also raised the issue of population-attributable risk. What proportion of violence in the population as a whole is due to mental illness? In other words, if mental illness were reduced, how much reduction would be seen in violence? A study in the United Kingdom found that the population-attributable risk for any personality disorder was 37 percent, for hazardous drinking it was 50 percent, and for antisocial personality disorder, 24 percent. Similar studies have found lower relative risk; mental illness is less important of a risk factor. Some studies suggest that substance use accounts for an increased risk, and others have found several risk factors related to violence, few of which are also related to mental illness.

Rosenberg closed by reiterating the four conclusions: the public perceives a strong association between mental illness and violence; rates of violence are increased but only moderately; only a small proportion of violence is attributable to mental health; and violence is variable with multiple causes and implications for treatment.

During the ensuing discussion, speakers raised additional issues around definitions. One issue is that there are no diagnostic categories for someone who is hostile all the time—there is a marked difference in the way angry affect is treated versus other types of affect. Another issue raised was measuring the adverse impact of exposure to violence on the mental health of children; violence prevention could be framed as mental health promotion in this respect.

NEUROCOGNITIVE MECHANISMS OF VIOLENT BEHAVIOR[6]

James Blair spoke about the neurocognitive systems that mediate or increase risk of interpersonal violence. He distinguished between two forms of interpersonal violence: reactive violence is frustration based or threat based, while instrumental violence is used to achieve a goal. Several mental health conditions increase the risk of reactive aggression, such as anxiety, borderline personality disorder, childhood bipolar disorder, depression, intermittent explosive disorder, and psychopathy. Whereas only one mental illness increases the risk of instrumental aggression—psychopathy (i.e., callous and unemotional [CU] traits). However, both types of aggression are normative behaviors; reactive aggression is the ultimate response to a

---

[6] This section summarizes information presented by James Blair, National Institute of Mental Health.

threat, and in some circumstances, instrumental aggression might be the appropriate decision to make.

Blair explained the brain mechanism responsible for reactive aggression, a threat-response circuitry that includes the amygdala hypothalamus and extends into the periaqueductal gray. This neurocognitive system generates the response to a threat: in the distance, it might cause a person to freeze; closer, it might cause flight; and in very close proximity, it might result in fighting. This process is somewhat regulated by various frontal systems, as well. It is also highly responsive to the amount of stimulation—from low, freeze, to high, fight. He suggested that this should mean that individuals who are at heightened risk for reactive aggression should also have a heightened responsiveness of this circuitry. In fact, this is the case in brain scans of people with PTSD and other disorders known to increase risk of reactive aggression. Trauma and neglect also increase the responsiveness of this threat circuitry, and problems of emotional regulation block the ability to reduce the responsiveness.

In terms of instrumental aggression, Blair pointed to a dysfunction in empathic responsiveness that increases risk. This dysfunction manifests clinically in CU traits, such as low pro-social emotions, including a lack of remorse or guilt, lack of empathy, or lack of attachment to other individuals. This brain circuitry includes the amygdala and the ventral medial prefrontal cortex, as well. The amygdala is responsible for basic socialization, such as learning how others react to one's actions. Depending on those reactions, one might choose to repeat or avoid that particular action in the future. However, if there is dysfunction in this circuitry, then there is an increase in CU traits and an inability to respond to the distress or pain of other individuals. Blair indicated that this inability to respond is not general, as there is no problem with recognizing anger or disgust.

A third brain mechanism described by Blair is a set of systems responsible for reward- and punishment-based decision making, which are not specifically related to CU traits. Problems in this circuitry tend to be prevalent across conduct disorders and to some extent in substance abuse populations. It also involves the amygdala, the ventral prefrontal cortex, and the caudate. Researchers have hypothesized, based on data from rat studies, that in the face of stimulus, a person might expect a positive outcome (i.e., reward) or a negative outcome (i.e., punishment). Normally, once a person determines which response will generate which outcome, he or she will continue the behavior that earns the reward. They learn to anticipate, or predict, which stimulus generates the reward and adapt their behavior accordingly when that feedback changes. However, in people with disruptive behavior or conduct disorder, this process does not occur. Additionally, those with conduct disorder show problems in the representation of value in the ventral medial prefrontal cortex. These issues are also seen in people with substance use disorders, ADHD, and externalizing disorders.

In summary, Blair noted that the three neurocognitive systems he discussed might have a relationship with certain disorders, but are not disorder specific. The acute threat response, if overly responsive, is more likely to have an episode of reactive aggression. If an individual has empathic problems, then he or she will not be as responsive to the distress or pain of others and is less likely to be inhibited in causing harm. And those with problems in the reward-and-punishment circuitry have issues with externalizing disorders.

He speculated that there are additional factors that affect brain processes, such as poverty, which modulates decision making, and impoverished diet, which affects the development of brain structures such as the amygdala. Genetics, too, might play a role in increased responsiveness in the acute threat circuitry, and possibly other systems. And finally, he mentioned the role of alcohol, which in healthy individuals reduces response to distress of others and affects reward–punishment decision making.

In the discussion following the presentation, Blair addressed a question regarding how suicide plays out in these neurocognitive systems by noting that it is difficult to determine because the brain architecture explored does not generate self-harm behavior in mammalian species. Impulsivity plays a role, but the process is not necessarily within one of the three systems he described. While reactive and instrumental aggression are different processes, what is reactive is subjective and lies within the perception of the perpetrator and his or her social milieu. He also discussed the implication of this research on treatment; presumably, treatments that teach pro-social behavior should recalibrate these systems in individuals with mental health conditions. This seems to be true in several cases, but he noted that conduct disorders, for example, might also require pharmacology.

REFERENCES

APA (American Psychiatric Association). 2013. *Diagnostic and statistical manual of mental disorders* (5th ed.). Arlington, VA: American Psychiatric Publishing.

CDC (Centers for Disease Control and Prevention) National Center for Injury Prevention and Control. 2005. Web-based Injury Statistics Query and Reporting System (WISQARS™). https://www.cdc.gov/injury/wisqars/index.html (accessed November 11, 2017).

Edgerton, R. 1966. Conceptions of psychosis in four East African societies. *American Anthropologist* 68(2):408–425.

Farmer, P. 2004. An anthropology of structural violence. *Current Anthropology* 5(3):307.

Hawton, K., and K. van Heeringen. 2009. Suicide. *The Lancet* 373(9672):1372–1381.

Jenkins, J. H. 1991. The state construction of affect: Political ethos and mental health among Salvadoran refugees. *Culture, Medicine, and Psychiatry* 15(2):139–165.

NIAAA (National Institute on Alcohol Abuse and Alcoholism). 2005. *National epidemiologic survey on alcohol and related conditions*. Rockville, MD: U.S. Department of Health and Human Services, National Institute on Alcohol Abuse and Alcoholism.

Nielssen, O. B., and M. M. Large. 2010. Rates of homicide during the first episode of psychosis and after treatment: A systematic review and meta-analysis. *Schizophrenia Bulletin* 36(4):702–712.

Nielssen, O. B., G. S. Malhi, P. D. McGorry, and M. M. Large. 2012. Overview of violence to self and others during the first episode of psychosis. *Journal of Clinical Psychiatry* 73(5):e580–e587.

NIMH (National Institute of Mental Health). 1991. *Epidemiologic catchment area survey of mental disorders, wave I (household), 1980–1985*. Rockville, MD: U.S. Department of Health and Human Services, National Institute of Mental Health.

Richardson, E. G., and D. Hemenway. 2011. Homicide, suicide, and unintentional firearm fatality: Comparing the United States with other high-income countries. *Journal of Trauma and Acute Care Surgery* 70(1):238–243.

Short, T., S. Thomas, P. Mullen, and J. R. Ogloff. 2013. Comparing violence in schizophrenia patients with and without comorbid substance-use disorders to community controls. *Acta Psychiatrica Scandinavica* 128(4):306–313.

Smith, T. W., P. V. Marsden, and M. Hout. 2013. *General social survey, 1972–2012*. Chicago, IL: National Opinion Research Center.

USSC (U.S. Sentencing Commission). 2011. *Guidelines manual*. Washington, DC: U.S. Sentencing Commission.

WHO (World Health Organization). 1996. *Violence: A public health priority*. Geneva, Switzerland: World Health Organization.

WHO. 2001. *Strengthening mental health promotion*. Fact sheet no. 220. Geneva, Switzerland: World Health Organization.

3

At the Intersection of Mental Health and Violence

The relationship between mental health and violence is complex and often misunderstood, with a number of misperceptions around risk of violence and victimization. Speakers discussed the stigma and discrimination that people with mental illness experience, particularly in the media. They also discussed the need for additional research on the intersection of mental health and violence, noting that the detection and the assessment of risk of violence are imprecise. Speakers also examined how a better understanding of the pathways for and the risk factors of violence could yield more effective interventions.

EXPERIENCES AND PERSPECTIVES RELATED TO MENTAL HEALTH AND VIOLENCE

Daniel Fisher of the Riverside Community Mental Health Center opened the panel titled "Experiences and Perspectives Related to Mental Health and Violence" by describing the importance of language. He noted that "patient" and "consumer" are not preferred terms within the community, and "survivor" is imprecise, and he suggested "people with lived experience" as a more inclusive and less discriminatory term. These issues, he stated, are not laboratory or clinical issues, but rather community and cultural issues. He emphasized that a more nuanced and accurate perspective of these lived experiences would help reduce stigma and provide better treatment options. For example, a peer-support recovery movement, similar to Alcoholics Anonymous, exists to provide nonmedical options for those with lived experience to connect and empower each other on the path to recovery.

Panelists further explored these issues within the context of the use of mechanical restraints, misperceptions around violence and its association with mental illness, as well as the history of deinstitutionalization and the failure to transition to community-based care.

Use of Restraints[1]

Because there is a misperception that people with mental illness are more prone to violence, it is a common practice to use mechanical restraints in institutional settings. But Elyn Saks asserted that the use of restraints, though well intentioned, is itself a violent act. Restraints when used over a length of time are extremely painful and degrading and cause feelings of helplessness. They can also be retraumatizing for those with posttraumatic stress disorder (PTSD) or for other survivors of trauma. She noted that, in her personal experience, the use of restraints was not necessarily due to her own behavior. In fact, the literature supports the idea that the use of restraints has more to do with the institutional ethos than other factors, such as patient characteristics or patient–staff ratio.

In exploring why restraints are used, Saks noted that there are studies that indicate that restraints help those being restrained feel safer. However, she observed that in her experience, she had never heard anyone express that sentiment, and that emergency fatalities do not lessen with the use of restraints. A second, more legitimate reason is that restraints can be protective for health care and service providers. For those patients who might become imminently violent, there is legitimate justification for restraints. However, she noted four reasons why the use of restraints as protection might be problematic:

- Restraints are often abused, despite statutes intended to prevent such abuse. She gave the example of one client she knew whose chart suggested restraints were used more for discipline than imminent violence.
- Imminent danger is difficult to predict, and patient and physician perspectives on a patient's own dangerousness vary widely on this.
- While well meaning, the use of restraints is an act of violence and can be more dangerous than not using them. Most staff injuries occur in the restraint process, which could indicate that the use of restraints itself causes people to be violent.
- There are often less restrictive alternatives available, such as the use of a padded cell.

---

[1] This section summarizes information presented by Elyn Saks, University of Southern California.

Saks suggested that restraints might cause more deaths than lives they save. In a series of articles in the *Hartford Courant*, a Harvard University statistician estimated that one to three people die each week in restraints—aspirating in their own vomit, strangling, or having heart attacks. She stated that since there are other means of protecting people, it is not clear whether restraints cost or save lives. Restraint-reduction efforts have resulted in lowered use of restraints without increased violence in Philadelphia and Massachusetts. The United Kingdom by and large does not use extreme restraints, and has not done so for 20 years.

In cases where the use of restraints might be justified (e.g., transporting a violent person or when a medical professional needs to be in close quarters), Saks recommended several enhanced procedural steps:

- Requiring 15-minute checks or an attempt to remove the restraints every hour
- Changing the liability scheme to make harm caused by restraints more liable (and harm caused by lack of restraint less liable)
- Providing guidelines to patients on behavior that will result in the removal of restraints
- Videotaping all restraint episodes
- Forbidding "spread eagle" restraint

In the discussion following Saks's presentation, workshop participants raised questions around the use of chemical restraints, particularly in the older population, and alternatives to restraints. Saks spoke of additional considerations around elderly populations, such as dementia and risk of falling. However, she stated that restraints are not always the answer—a person sitting with the patient could also provide assistance. Another audience member mentioned the use of a hospital bed programmed to alert staff if the patient tried to get up.

Impact of Violence on People with Mental Illness[2]

Harvey Rosenthal spoke about the impact of violence on the community of people with mental illness, particularly the fallout after horrific episodes of "active shooter" violence. The stigma and the misinformation around the role mental illness plays in violence is often heightened after incidents of mass violence, with resounding repercussions. Rosenthal mentioned that policies are often promoted in government that seek to respond to these incidents, but instead result in depersonalization and

---

[2] This section summarizes information presented by Harvey Rosenthal, New York Association of Psychiatric Rehabilitation Services, Inc.

criminalization of people with mental illness, and threaten to undo progress in promoting recovery, dignity, and integration.

One challenge that Rosenthal raised is that mental illness is loosely defined, particularly in the general population. Some people consider autism a mental illness (it falls instead under the rubric of developmental disability). A recent Kansas ruling in the Supreme Court places sex offenses under mental illness. And others consider sociopathy and substance abuse to be mental illnesses. At the same time, the common perception that one must be "crazy" to commit horrific acts confuses matters further and feeds into the misperception that mental illness is a risk factor for violence.

Rosenthal reiterated the fact that people with mental illness are at most marginally more violent than the general public. He noted that only 4 percent of violent crimes are affiliated with mental illness, and that 1 in 70,000 people with mental illness are committing murder of strangers (Swanson, 2015). To put it another way, of the 140,000 people in New York who are deemed "seriously and persistently mentally ill," two of them are at risk of committing murder. Additional research has concluded that there is no clear relationship between psychiatric diagnosis and mass murder, and that most mass murderers are young men with no diagnosis of psychosis (Fox, 2015). Despite these facts, the perception of the link between mental illness and violence has policy consequences, such as campaigns to force medication and other treatment on people. In New York, Rosenthal stated, the law now mandates that mental health professionals report if a patient who owns a gun expresses anger.

On the other hand, people with mental illnesses are 11 times more likely to be victims of violence and 5 times more likely to be murder victims. And, yet, Rosenthal asserted, the public discourse still revolves around the harm potentially committed by people with mental illness, and not the potential harm faced by the vulnerable. In particular, there are efforts to promote forced-treatment laws, despite the previously cited lack of evidence on a link between mental illness and violence.

Rosenthal did share some positive items that have come about recently regarding mental illness and violence. In particular, the Associated Press (AP) created guidelines for its reporters on writing about incidents in which people with mental illness might be involved:

- Do not describe an individual as mentally ill unless pertinent to the story and the diagnosis is properly sourced.
- Do not use derogatory terms such as "insane," "crazy," "nuts," or "deranged."
- Do not assume that mental illness is a factor in violent crime.
- Do not use descriptions that denote pity, such as "afflicted with."

He closed by discussing the implications of a "broken system," a commonly used term with different meanings for different stakeholders. For consumers, it is disempowering, dependency fostering, and overly focused on medication. For families, it is a lack of assistance with their loved ones. For others, it means more forced treatment. And for the media and much of the general public, it means unchecked violence. To fix this, he suggested that a new narrative needs to be created—one that is focused on both the facts and the nuance around mental health and violence, and one that gives voice to people with mental illness.

Reflecting on Mental Health and Violence[3]

Robert Bernstein observed that people with mental illness have endured a long history of segregation and discrimination. In 1990, the Americans with Disabilities Act (ADA) was passed with the intention of "mainstreaming" people with disabilities, including mental illness. The ADA was a sea change in the treatment of people with mental illness, away from the previous approach of mandatory institutionalization and custodial care toward a focus on community inclusion and multimodal treatment. In 1999, the U.S. Supreme Court ruled that, per the ADA, unwarranted institutional confinement was a form of segregation and that public systems have an obligation to provide integrated services where feasible.

This is of course an ongoing discourse, Bernstein stated, but there are profound reforms occurring to improve situations for people with mental illness. In particular, deinstitutionalization was the cornerstone for a mental health civil rights movement that preceded the ADA, and one that is still an important element today. In the 1960s and the 1970s, deinstitutionalization was the first wave of reform and was based on the terrible conditions in state hospitals, where patients were not only incarcerated but also routinely put in restraints. Given that most people with mental illness are not a danger to themselves or others, and that the institutions themselves raised other problematic issues, Bernstein asserted that deinstitutionalization was a positive goal.

However, he was careful to point out that integration of patients with communities was intended to be accompanied by a comprehensive community mental health movement, in which services are community based rather than hospital based. Yet, this movement never materialized, and as a result of poor funding, the mental health domain today exists as a crisis system. People with serious mental illness have suffered, and perceptions of mental illness have suffered as well.

---

[3] This section summarizes information presented by Robert Bernstein, Judge David L. Bazelon Center for Mental Health Law.

The community mental health movement was intended to provide services to anyone with mental illness, but today it operates solely for those who pose a danger. Because of a lack of funding, Bernstein stated, there is little investment in prevention and early intervention with a primary focus on emergency response. The current mental health system, he noted, is an upstream system failure—the development of a mental health crisis being evidence of a lack of early intervention. He closed by noting that because of this systematic lack of funding where it is most needed for long-term solutions, there is a perverse incentive now to capitalize on public perceptions of mental health and violence if it means greater resource allocation for mental health.

Discussion

Following the presentations, panelists and workshop participants discussed additional issues raised, including challenges outside the United States. In Latin America and the Caribbean, the movement toward recovery and integration is not nearly as robust. Fisher and Rosenthal both noted that the recovery movement has its roots in the United States, and it is important that, even while expanding it outside the United States, continued work and sustained commitment is maintained at its origin.

Additionally, Eric Caine of the University of Rochester Medical Center expanded on the issue of community mental health, observing that one of the reasons for its lack of prioritization and funding was a change in the way mental health was structured and treated. Caine went on to note that, previously, community mental health fell under the purview of the National Institute of Mental Health, but currently the Substance Abuse and Mental Health Services Administration (SAMHSA) provides block grants to states, with individual counties developing systems and allocating funds. At this level of granularity, he postulated, grassroots and peer-led organizations have an important role in shaping community mental health.

DETECTING AND ASSESSING MENTAL HEALTH DYSFUNCTION AND RISK FOR VIOLENCE

Detection of risk of violence is currently an imprecise science, speakers observed, that could benefit from greater study and refinement. One of the major challenges faced is that violence is not a high-probability event, and statistically the percentage of violent people is low. Risk factors for violence are also varied, and it is unclear which factors and in which combination might result in a violent act. With current instruments, this results in inaccurate assessment of risk, which carries implications for those with mental illness and those with a propensity for violence. Speakers discussed these challenges and approaches to develop more refined instruments.

Violence Risk Assessment[4]

Seena Fazel spoke about risk assessment for interpersonal violence by providing an overview, synthesizing evidence, and reflecting on implications and next steps. Violence assessments, he stated, range from unstructured clinical opinion to validated instruments that use tools as proxies for clinical judgment. There are some 200 of these instruments in existence, and they are widely used in forensic psychiatric services and criminal justice settings. Often, they are used to make decisions about sentencing, parole, and probation. Assessments that combine elements of structured and unstructured approaches, such as actuarial instruments to calculate a probability score, or categorizing risk as high, medium, or low based on a predetermined checklist of risk factors, are commonly used.

Fazel and his colleagues examined the literature and located 40 systematic reviews and meta-analyses on commonly used tools to determine their evidence base. They found a number of problems with these studies, including a failure to exclude duplicates (resulting in overestimation of effects) or to explore heterogeneity (resulting in wide variance). They found six studies that actually examined predictive validity; five of those explored only the PCL-R (Psychopathy Checklist), and one looked at another instrument.

Because of this lack of comprehensive evidence, they ran their own meta-analysis, which also included previously unpublished data. This resulted in a large study of 73 samples with about 24,000 individuals who underwent risk assessment by 1 of the 9 most commonly used tools. The outcomes were presented in a few different ways, but Fazel singled out the positive predictive value (PPV) in particular, because of its clinical usefulness. PPV is an assessment of how well the instrument identifies true positives—that is, "if an instrument determines high risk, how many of those people go on to violently offend or sexually offend?" he explained. Per the meta-analysis, the PPV for "violent offending" was 0.41, meaning the majority of those determined to be high risk did not, in fact, go on to commit violence. At the same time, the analysis showed a PPV of 0.91 for the low-risk group determination, suggesting the tools were better at assessing those who would not go on to commit violence[5] (Fazel et al., 2012).

Fazel noted that how well the instruments perform is highly dependent on their use. The PPV for determining violent offense suggested that they were not great at predicting violence and therefore were not suitable for decisions such as sentencing or release from hospital. Looking at other

---

[4] This section summarizes information presented by Seena Fazel, University of Oxford, United Kingdom.

[5] A PPV of 0.41 indicated that of those in the high-risk group, only 41 percent went on to commit violence. However, a PPV of 0.91 indicated that 91 percent of the time, the test was correct in determining an individual was in the low-risk group (Fazel et al., 2012).

outcomes from the meta-analysis, Fazel noted there was some evidence that the instruments could inform treatment and management plans and could be used to screen out low-risk individuals. In comparing them to other tools, Fazel observed that they fared poorly compared with diagnostic tools but were more similar to existing prognostic tools from other medical disciplines. However, the consequences of moderately useful tools in violence prevention are different: There are costs in terms of extended detention, as well as costs of staff training and time.

In a second review, Fazel and his colleagues looked more closely at different tools specifically designed for populations with mental illness. He noted that they were disappointing due to wide variation in their predictive ability. Additionally, only two studies looked at schizophrenia, which would normally be considered a risk factor for violence. In looking at the content of the tools, he and his team determined there is a wide variation in what is included; for example, the instruments included a wide variety of factors related to criminal history, failing to converge on what that entailed. And in another recent study by Jeremy Coid and his colleagues, these instruments were found to fare even more poorly with psychopathy than they do with mental illness (Coid et al., 2013).

Fazel concluded his remarks with a summary of his findings. The risk assessment tools he examined had limited value in predicting risk of reoffending but could be useful in identifying different risk groups for management. More importantly, he argued that the tools should be used differently: to screen out low-risk people as a means of focusing resources on the remainder. He also felt that the research could be better improved—by independent funding, validation by impartial experts, and higher standards of evidence—toward the development of better assessment tools.

Strategies for Preventing Youth Violence[6]

Serious violence, Dustin Pardini observed, peaks in adolescence. Most youth who engage in violence cease over time, and only a small percentage persist into adulthood. In his presentation, he focused on programs implemented during elementary school, before children display seriously violent behavior. Universal interventions are delivered to an entire population of youth, while selected programs target youth with population-level or demographic risk factors, such as living in a high-crime neighborhood. Indicated interventions, which represent a large percentage of interventions, focus on children who exhibit early forms of violent behavior, such as physical fighting, or characteristics of oppositional defiant disorder and conduct disorder.

---

[6] This section summarizes information presented by Dustin Pardini, University of Pittsburgh.

In a recent meta-analysis, effect sizes demonstrated that indicated interventions produced the greatest reduction in aggressive behavior, most likely because these youth are already showing high levels of aggression (Wilson et al., 2003). The effects get smaller as the intervention becomes more general, though they still remain significant. So which approach is better? On the one hand, the identification of high-risk individuals who will commit violence is difficult. Instead, the focus should be on reducing the risk in the population as a whole. The benefit per individual would be small, but everyone would be included in the intervention. On the other hand, some research indicates that a small number of juvenile offenders actually commit a large amount of youth violence. Focusing on those adolescents would have optimal impact on the overall amount of crime.

Pardini noted that both approaches have their advantages and disadvantages, but he suggested that further exploration of how best to implement targeted interventions was important, particularly the process of screening youth for the programs. An effective screening instrument needs to be brief, psychometrically reliable, precise, and administered across multiple settings. Most importantly, it should significantly predict future violence and have evidence to show such. Because violence is a relatively low-probability event, a risk-screening instrument will generate a higher number of false positives.

There are several practical implications of making errors with the instrument, Pardini emphasized. Where the line is drawn between high and low risk, or when there is a false positive, makes the difference between a child being placed in the intervention or not. This could have negative ramifications for the child because of the labeling, as well. Also, there is some evidence to suggest that grouping children into such interventions could result in deviancy training, in which there is take-up of adverse outcomes instead of prevention. False positives are also a poor use of funds, and false negatives reduce the impact of the program.

Currently, there are no standardized empirically based risk-assessment tools for screening youth to refer them to targeted programs. There are a few ad hoc tools, but none that are available for the general population. These ad hoc tools are based on the idea that early conduct problems are strong predictors for future violent behavior, an association seen in longitudinal studies. In an analysis of these risk-assessment tools, Pardini and his colleagues determined that they were mediocre at accurately identifying high-risk youth, with a large number of false positives, especially among girls. This is not surprising, because as Pardini previously explained, violence peaks in adolescence and ceases over time. Only a small number of violent youth persist in their violence.

The Pittsburgh Youth Survey, which began in 1986, was an attempt to develop a more accurate risk-assessment tool (van Wijk et al., 2005).

Researchers followed a sample of children from public schools in Pittsburgh over time. The children were questioned at specific points about their violent behavior, and official criminal records were also collected. Among the sample, the rates of violence were high, echoing concerns about a disproportionate impact of violence on minority youth. Pardini and his colleagues looked at all of the risk factors at the first assessment point—not just behavioral issues, but also family conditions, peer influence, and neighborhood characteristics, among others. They identified 51 risk factors, and using statistical regression, found the 11 strongest, ranging from academic issues to physical aggression to family poverty. These risk factors demonstrate better sensitivity and specificity than many adult assessment tools, but Pardini felt there was room for improvement. He proposed examining multiple datasets across the country and conducting comparable analyses to replicate factors measured by parents, teachers, and the children themselves. Once they have identified those factors that consistently predict violence, they plan to develop standardized item content to assess each risk domain. The final step would be the development of a psychometric tool with as brief a measure as possible that can be administered across multiple settings.

Impact of Bullying and Mental Health[7]

Dieter Wolke opened his presentation by remarking that bullying has a definition in common language, but also a scientific construction that goes beyond conduct problems. He emphasized that while conflict among children teaches them how to resolve conflicts, bullying is not about conflict resolution but about power and intentional harmdoing. There are different types of bullying, such as overt bullying, relational bullying, and cyberbullying.

Wolke identified four groups associated with bullying:

- Pure bully, who perpetrates the aggression but never becomes a victim
- Pure victim, who gets bullied but never bullies others
- Bully-victim, who bullies at times and is bullied at other times
- Neutral child, who can be a bystander or a defender

From where does bullying stem? In evolutionary biology, bullying could be a means of accessing resources and gaining dominance in a hierarchy. In fact, bullying could be protective against having to fight all the time. If this is true, Wolke posited, then it should be seen in all socioeconomic status

---

[7] This section summarizes the information presented by Dieter Wolke, University of Warwick, United Kingdom.

groups, but would be more frequent the scarcer the resources. In a recent meta-analysis, Wolke and his colleague concluded that, indeed, bullying is found in all classes and segments in society (Tippett and Wolke, 2014). In another meta-analysis, researchers discovered that bullying is more prevalent in more unequal societies, so that inequality as a proxy for scarcity is in fact correlated with bullying occurrence (Elgar et al., 2009).

Adverse consequences of bullying have been explored in the literature, and Wolke shared some examples. In one study in primary school, Wolke and his colleagues looked at physical and emotional health problems in the four previously mentioned bully groups. He noted that the most strongly affected group is the bully-victims, who are somewhat socially defeated. Those with the lowest problems are the pure bullies, who are not victims of bullying themselves (Wolke et al., 2001). In a longitudinal study on bullying history, researchers found that incidence of bullying is not the only factor—chronic bullying has add-on effects. Those who are currently being bullied fare worse than those who were bullied in the past, but those bullied currently and in the past do worst of all (Bogart et al., 2014).

In another study with far-reaching implications, researchers in Britain discovered that bullying in elementary school was associated with self-harm with intent to commit suicide at age 17, with a population-attributable fraction of 20 percent (Lereya et al., 2013). This means that if bullying were eliminated, Wolke explained, 20 percent of adolescent self-harm cases could be prevented. He emphasized the importance of this by noting that, by comparison, obesity, which commands significant resources for its prevention, only accounts for 3 percent of heart attacks. Other research supports similar findings; another study found that chronic bullying before age 11 increases risk of psychotic experiences threefold (Wolke et al., 2014).

In studies done in adults who experienced bullying as children, researchers again found health problems, particularly psychological conditions, in those who were pure victims, but also bully-victims. They had poorer psychosocial outcomes, as well, including difficulty maintaining employment and relationships (Copeland et al., 2013; Wolke et al., 2014). In another study looking at inflammatory responses to C-reactive protein, the stronger or more chronic the bullying, the higher the response. The largest change was for victims, followed by bully-victims, but the lowest was in pure bullies (Copeland et al., 2014).

Wolke closed his remarks by summarizing the findings from the literature: being bullied has wide-ranging effects on mental health, from increasing risk for psychopathology to adverse psychosocial and social outcomes. The chronically bullied and bully-victims have the worst long-term outcomes. Bullies do not experience these adverse outcomes but do tend to show lower empathy and higher rates of manipulation as adults.

Bullying is highly prevalent, affecting 15 to 20 percent of the population, and affects all social strata. In the United Kingdom, the majority of children who have not attended school for a whole year have not done so because of bullying. Bullying's impacts extend beyond the individual and his or her long-term outcomes, but also has an impact on society through workplace productivity. Policies that address bullying, Wolke asserted, will have a universal impact.

Discussion

In response to questions regarding mental illness risk factors for youth violence, Pardini noted that the main driving predictors are conduct disorders and oppositional defiant disorder; others, such as depression and anxiety, do not have a strong relationship. Additionally, when he and his colleagues analyzed other potential factors, such as trauma and physical abuse and neglect at home, they were also not as significant in predicting future violent behavior.

A related topic raised in discussion between panelists and the audience was the role of the family in bullying. In response to one such question, Wolke noted that over time, children spend more time with their peers than their family members, emphasizing the importance of peer acceptance. He went on to explain that while violence by parents is detrimental to a child's well-being, most violence experienced is by peers and siblings. However, violence among siblings is rarely considered abuse or bullying. But Wolke noted that sibling violence has adverse effects, particularly in regard to bullying—those who are victimized in their own home by a sibling are 4 to 12 times more likely to be a victim at school, as well. And those who bully their siblings are three times more likely to bully others.

Participants at the workshop also further explored challenges raised by screening, including the important distinction between a diagnosis and a positive screen, the latter of which has been shown to decrease productivity. Additionally, screening in schools raises issues around data protection. The combination of a false-positive screen and potential privacy concerns has profound negative implications for individuals.

Finally, in a discussion around criminalization of sibling abuse, bullying, and other violent youth behavior, panelists and several audience participants raised skepticism around the effectiveness of criminalizing people. While some bullying and family violence would under other circumstances be considered crimes, families and schools are often reluctant to report such incidents. In addition, several participants noted that rehabilitation and treatment have a greater positive impact than criminalization in both other-directed and self-directed violence.

REFERENCES

Bogart, L., M. Elliott, D. Klein, S. Tortolero, S. Mrug, M. Peskin, S. Davies, E. Schink, and M. Schuster. 2014. Peer victimization in fifth grade and health in tenth grade. *Pediatrics* 133(3):440–447.

Coid, J., S. Ullrich, and C. Kallis. 2013. Predicting future violence among individuals with psychopathy. *British Journal of Psychiatry* 203(5):387–388.

Copeland, W. E., S. Wolke, and A. Angold. 2013. Adult psychiatric and suicide outcomes of bullying and being bullied by peers in childhood adolescence. *JAMA Psychiatry* 70(4):419–426.

Copeland, W. E., D. Wolke, S. T. Lereya, L. Shanahan, C. Worthman, and E. J. Costello. 2014. Childhood bullying involvement predicts low-grade systemic inflammation into adulthood. *Proceedings of the National Academy of Sciences of the United States of America* 111(21):7570–7575.

Elgar, F. J., W. Craig, W. Boyce, A. Morgan, and R. Vella-Zarb. 2009. Income inequality and school bullying: Multilevel study of adolescents in 37 countries. *Journal of Adolescent Health* 45(4):351–359.

Fazel, S., J. P. Singh, H. Doll, and M. Grann. 2012. Use of risk assessment instruments to predict violence and antisocial behavior in 73 samples involving 24,827 people: Systematic review and meta-analysis. *British Medical Journal* 345:e4692.

Fox, J. 2015. *Extreme killing*. Thousand Oaks, CA: SAGE Publications.

Lereya, S. T., C. Winsper, J. Heron, G. Lewis, D. Gunnell, H. Fisher, and D. Wolke. 2013. Being bullied during childhood and the prospective pathways to self-harm in late adolescence. *Journal of the American Academy of Child & Adolescent Psychiatry* 52(6):608–618.

Swanson, J. 2015. Mental illness and reduction of gun violence and suicide: Bringing epidemiologic research to policy. *Annals of Epidemiology* 25(5):366–376.

Tippett, N., and D. Wolke. 2014. Socioeconomic status and bullying: A meta-analysis. *American Journal of Public Health* 104(6):e48–e59.

van Wijk, A., R. Loeber, R. Vermeiren, D. Pardini, R. Bullens, and T. Doreleijers. 2005. Violent juvenile sex offenders compared with violence juvenile nonsex offenders: Explorative findings from the Pittsburgh Youth Study. *Sexual Abuse: A Journal of Research and Treatment* 17(3):333–352.

Wilson, S. J., M. W. Lipsey, and J. H. Derzon. 2003. The effects of school-based intervention programs on aggressive behavior: A meta-analysis. *Journal of Consulting and Clinical Psychology* 71(1):136–149.

Wolke, D., S. Woods, K. Stanford, and H. Schulz. 2001. Bullying and victimization of primary school children in England and Germany: Prevalence and school factors. *British Journal of Psychology* 92:673–696.

Wolke, D., S.T. Lereya, H.L. Fisher, G. Lewis, and S. Zammit. 2014. Bullying in elementary school and psychotic experiences at 18 years: A longitudinal, population-based cohort study. *Psychological Medicine* 44(10):2199–2211.

4

Means and Modifiers

Despite advances in the science of violence prevention, several gaps and challenges remain. The impact of violence is mediated through several means, such as firearms and pesticides, and modifiers, such as alcohol. Specifically, the lethality of firearms and commonly used pesticides result in higher fatalities, while alcohol reduces inhibitions that might otherwise be a barrier to violence. Speakers presented on how these means and modifiers affect violence and violence prevention, and how reducing access to these means can reduce violence.

RESTRICTING THE MEANS OF VIOLENCE

Speakers discussed issues around the access to lethal means of violence and successful methods to reduce such access, particularly among those with mental illness. Speakers also noted, however, that such violence tends to be self-directed rather than other-directed. As noted by other speakers in the workshop, people with mental illness are not at higher risk of interpersonal violence compared with the general population, but their risk of self-directed violence is much higher. Thus, speakers discussed how restricting access to lethal means could be a method of reducing the incidence of suicide and self-directed harm.

Firearms Means Restriction and Mental Health[1]

Daniel Webster considered the research on firearms prohibitions on people with mental illness. A study conducted by Jeff Swanson in Connecticut analyzed data from public mental health and criminal justice agencies, providing a sample of 23,000 individuals with severe mental illness (Swanson et al., 2013). Criteria for severe mental illness included diagnosis and hospitalization for schizophrenia, bipolar disorder, and major depressive disorder. The study focused on two general cohorts: one had at least one of four potential mental illness disqualifications for firearms possession, the other had no disqualifications. Of the overall sample, only 5 percent were disqualified because of severe mental illness. In 2007, the state began recording these disqualifications. The study compared the rates of violence in both groups before and after the onset of reporting. Swanson and his colleagues found an odds ratio of 0.69; essentially, there was a 31 percent reduction in risk for arrest of violent crime because of the reporting, while those who were not affected by reporting had no change in offending (Swanson et al., 2013). Webster pointed out that while crime in this study involved more than just gun-related incidents, it still showed a significant impact on gun-related crime. Other studies looking at interpersonal violence and other mental health issues, including substance abuse, also show that mental-illness-related prohibitions reduce violence in those two groups. In particular, one study looked at perpetrators of intimate partner violence and found reductions in homicide associated with firearm restrictions for those with restraining orders (Vigdor and Mercy, 2006).

However, most of the risk related to mental health and violence is around self-harm and access to lethal means. Webster noted that there is a common perception that someone with intent of suicide will find a way to do so regardless of available methods. In contrast, several historical examples of restriction of lethal means and subsequent reduction of suicide. For example, the removal of coal ovens in British homes reduced suicides by one-third, and raising the barrier on the Duke Ellington Bridge in Washington, DC, reduced suicides by one-half. The success of a suicide attempt is also related to the lethality of the method. Despite the high availability of means such as rope, knives, and poison, these make up a lower percentage of the case fatality rate compared with firearms.

Bringing these two factors together suggests that suicide risk associated with access to lethal means is higher. In a national study, Doug Weibe found that, controlling for other factors, risk is elevated threefold when there is a gun in the home (Wiebe, 2003), a finding shown in other research as well.

---

[1] This section summarizes information presented by Daniel Webster, Johns Hopkins Bloomberg School of Public Health.

Other studies, both cross-sectional and longitudinal, that look at the population level have found a positive association with prevalence of firearms ownership and risk of suicide, with higher risks at younger ages[2] (Miller et al., 2007; Stevens et al., 2006). On a similar note, an analysis of gun ownership rates in the 1990s and youth suicide rates showed that suicides decreased dramatically as household gun rates dropped.

Regarding restricting firearms access to youth, the laws that require owners to lock guns away reduced suicide risk among 14- to 17-year-olds by 8 percent overall. Additional laws related to restricting firearms did not have an effect, though, nor did they have an effect on older youth aged 22 to 24 years[3] (Webster et al., 2004). Other studies support these findings, showing protective effects for older individuals with the Brady Handgun Violence Prevention Act and some state laws that require permits for purchasing (Andrés and Hempstead, 2011).

Means Restriction and Suicide[4]

Suicide accounts for 60 percent of all violent deaths in men, and 75 percent in women, globally. In high-income countries, more than 80 percent of violent deaths are suicide. In sub-Saharan Africa and Latin America, suicide accounts for a lower proportion of violent deaths, but in Asia and Eastern Europe, suicide accounts for more than half of violent deaths. Of all suicides globally, 84 percent occur in low- and middle-income countries. China and India account for 56 percent of all male suicides and 61 percent of all female suicides. However, most of the research and intervention models on suicide prevention come from high-income countries.

In both China and India, 50 percent of suicides are due to poison, usually pesticides or rodent poisons, both of which are lethal. In a study that looked at suicides globally, researchers found that one-third used poison, usually found in the home (Gunnell et al., 2007). Phillips described a few characteristics of pesticide poisoning and suicide in China:

- Relative to other methods, it is lethal—6 percent of those who end up in the emergency department die, versus 1 percent of those who use other methods.
- 43 percent of those who use pesticides thought about the attempt for less than 5 minutes, compared with 16 percent of those who

---

[2] Difference in suicide rates for 1 percentage point higher in household firearm ownership in state, 2000–2002 (Miller et al., 2007; Stevens et al., 2006).

[3] Estimates for youth-focused firearm laws on suicide rates among ages 14 to 17 years (Webster et al., 2004).

[4] This section summarizes information presented by Michael Phillips, Shanghai Jiao Tong University School of Medicine.

used other methods of suicide; this is partly because of the ready availability of such pesticides.
- Those who use pesticides tend to have low intent to die, which contradicts the popular opinion that those who are more intent on dying use more lethal methods.
- Only 33 percent of those who ingest a pesticide had a diagnosis of mental illness at the time, compared with 54 percent of those who use other methods.

Michael Phillips emphasized that last point by addressing "common knowledge" in the West that suicide is an outcome of mental illness. From their research, Phillips and his colleagues observed that more than 60 percent of those who attempt suicide do not in fact have mental illness, and using psychological autopsy, they found that 30 percent of those who died of suicide did not have a mental illness.

Regions in China where pesticides are stored in homes have higher rates of suicide than regions where pesticides are less likely to be stored at home. At the same time, as China's population has increasingly urbanized, with fewer people working in agriculture, access to pesticides has dropped, and suicides have reduced. Phillips remarked that there are 100,000 fewer suicides in China per year than 20 years ago. He hypothesized that in low- and middle-income countries with a large agricultural sector, patterns of pesticide access and use might be a more useful approach to suicide reduction than prevalence and treatment rates of mental disorders. As such, he proposed a set of strategies to address suicide by pesticide poisoning:

- Banning the most toxic compounds
- Decreasing access to pesticides in the home
- Community education about the lethality of these chemicals and about appropriate storage
- Improved training and increased access to necessary drugs and equipment for rural primary care health providers

While improving medical knowledge and treatment and raising community awareness are important, Phillips asserted that means restriction should be the main focus of efforts to reduce suicide. The effectiveness of means restriction, however, is dependent on how feasible the restriction is, and what the proportion of deaths that particular method comprises. It also depends on whether a substitution method is available. As an example, Phillips described a study in Sri Lanka in which a more lethal chemical was substituted for one that was banned; yet, when the importation of highly toxic pesticides was completely banned, the suicide rate dropped dramatically. He cautioned that a means-restriction approach should be constantly monitored for these and other types of mediating factors.

Phillips also suggested additional large-scale interventions for restricting means:

- Promote secure storage in homes, fields, or a centralized community location
- Establish a minimum pesticide list, so individuals may only own certain pesticides
- Promote integrated pest management programs
- Apply a tax to pesticides that increases with pesticide lethality
- Limit usage of pesticides in each village or community to a small number of licensed individuals who would apply pesticides for all community members
- Train pesticide retailers to recognize potentially suicidal individuals
- Limit sale of pesticides to single-use amounts

Phillips closed with a description of a project he and his colleagues implemented in Shaanxi province in China. The objective of the project was to promote the installation of 10,000 lockboxes for the storage of pesticides. An educational campaign was also rolled out and suicide rates before and after the intervention were monitored and compared with other townships without the intervention. The lockboxes had two keys, with the idea that two people (usually husband and wife) were required to open the box. Researchers followed the families over 3 years to assess compliance. They found that there was limited uptake of the intervention—about 20 to 30 percent. People were using the box, but few were using the locks. When the educational component stopped, use of the locks dropped: 88 percent were using the box, but almost none of them were locking it after the 3-year period. Ultimately, they did see a drop in suicide rates in the intervention areas—about 23 percent—while the rates in the control sites increased by 2 percent. Phillips observed that 100 percent compliance is unreasonable to expect, and means restriction needs to be part of a larger overall suicide prevention strategy. Yet, he noted that in low- and middle-income countries, focusing on individual-level mental health approaches might not be the best use of resources.

Regulation and Means Restriction[5]

Mike Luo described issues raised by several news stories he wrote regarding gun violence and mental illness. In particular, in examining mass

---

[5] This section summarizes information presented by Mike Luo, *The New York Times*.

violence events, such as one in which a disturbed young man opened fire on a crowd, killing several people, he questioned what it meant for people with mental illness to have access to firearms. He noted that the current federal standard stipulates that one cannot purchase or possess firearms if one has been involuntarily committed or adjudicated as "mentally defective." The vast majority of those with mental illness, even severe mental illness, will never get to this point. Luo and his colleagues wanted to explore this area further to learn the stories of people with diagnosed mental illness who possessed firearms. However, he noted, there was a big privacy challenge in this area, dealing with both mental health and gun ownership.

In most states, he observed, records of purchases of concealed handgun permits are not publicly available. Because he was unable to obtain such records via public inquiries, he instead inquired at police departments and courts for records of people from whom firearms were confiscated for mental health reasons. Such calls are not enough to disqualify someone from possessing firearms but are usually grounds for temporary confiscation because a person is a danger to himself or herself or to others. However, the circumstances under which it is legal to confiscate a firearm are not straightforward. Luo noted that while taking away a firearm on someone's person is usually allowable, the situation is less clear when the firearm is in another location. Most police departments would require a warrant to confiscate the weapon in these circumstances; for example, Connecticut and Indiana passed laws giving police more leeway on this.

In the past year in Connecticut, there were 180 instances when police removed firearms from people they deemed to pose a risk of imminent danger, 40 percent of which involved serious mental illness. In 2012, Luo and his colleagues found that in Marion County, Indiana, there were 30 instances of confiscation, with about 40 percent of those involving mental illness. Most people were placed under observation, but not involuntarily committed, and in most instances, the firearms were returned shortly.

Luo cited a few examples of these policies at work. In Indianapolis, before the law giving police greater jurisdiction was passed, an individual with a diagnosis of schizophrenia retook possession of his firearm and was later involved in a police shooting. In Hillsborough County, Florida, there was another instance in which a veteran with a history of treatment for depression, anxiety, and paranoia made violence-related comments to his psychiatrist and subsequently had his firearms confiscated. He was involuntarily hospitalized but not committed, and a few months later had his firearms returned. In a third situation in Colorado, an individual with prior suicide attempts, who also had not been committed, had successfully requested his firearms be returned.

In the context of these cases, Luo raised a series of questions about the intersection of privacy, regulation, public health, science, and rights. Given that involuntary commitment is a difficult process, where is the standard set for disqualification of possession of firearms? Should there be a protocol for restoring rights, and what should it look like? What is the best way to predict future violence by a person with mental illness and in possession of a gun? Where is the line between Second Amendment rights and public health and safety?

Discussion

In the subsequent discussion, workshop participants shared their perspectives on issues raised during the presentations, particularly around predicting future violence and restricting lethal means. Webster noted that, rather than focusing on diagnosis or involuntary commitment to disqualify an individual from owning a lethal weapon, the focus should be on potential danger. For example, indicators of substance abuse, such as multiple violations for driving under the influence of alcohol (DUIs), magnify risk associated with severe mental illness. Mark Rosenberg of The Task Force for Global Health agreed, and he suggested that stress and distress are triggers for suicide and could be assessed.

Phillips echoed comments made earlier, stating that predicting individual behavior is very difficult, and current instruments to do so are imprecise. Luo concurred, mentioning that most assessments of risk are conducted by psychiatrists using unstructured criteria.

Eric Caine of the University of Rochester Medical Center considered whether community-based approaches, in which all members of the community feel invested, might be a more effective means of reducing violence. He spoke about a program in King County, Washington, in which a coalition was built among public health officials, injury prevention stakeholders, and firearms retailers. The program involves incentivizing firearms buyers to purchase gun locks by offering discounts. It does not ask anyone to serve as a gatekeeper, but instead builds a community of safety. Caine suggested that such an approach might help bridge differences among different stakeholders.

ALCOHOL, ALCOHOL USE DISORDERS, AND VIOLENCE

Alcohol's impact on violence is observable but not fully understood. Speakers discussed insights from experimental and observational studies that explore the neurobiological and sociological pathways of alcohol-mediated violence. They also discussed gaps in policies, both in the United States and around the world, including those related to lack of funding and political and social will.

Escalated Aggression in Rodent Models: Novel Brain Mechanisms for Alcohol[6]

Evidence suggests that alcohol plays a significant role in violence, but the relationship is complicated, Klaus Miczek explained. For example, two-thirds of all violence involves alcohol: 86 percent of homicides, 60 percent of sexual offenses, 75 percent of spousal abuse, and 30 percent of assault offenders report using alcohol.

In the 1980s, a watershed discovery illuminated the mechanism by which alcohol affects the brain, which caused a shift toward focusing on specific proteins, such as glutamate, GABA, and serotonin. He noted that alcohol has a biphasic dose-effect: at low and acute doses it has pro-aggressive effects, and at high doses it is anti-aggressive. Alcohol withdrawal also causes aggression; the greater the exposure to alcohol, the more intense the withdrawal and the more intense the aggressive episodes. However, the impact of alcohol on individuals is highly variable. In a certain subset of individuals, alcohol causes a large change in aggressive behavior. Miczek asked, "Who are these individuals, how can they be identified, and can they be corrected?"

In mouse studies, researchers have observed that some mice display large increases in aggressive behavior, as well as a change in the pattern of that behavior. In an animal that consumes water, the typical pattern for biting is in the rump. For those who ingest alcohol, the shift in target is dramatic: not only are they biting more frequently, but the bites themselves cause greater injury.

Miczek expounded further on the mechanisms by which these behavior shifts occur:

- **Dopamine.** Aggression produces dangers, but it also produces satisfaction and pleasure associated with rewards. In animal studies, it is possible to measure neurochemical events before, during, and after an aggressive act, as well as during recovery. In anticipation of an aggressive episode, dopamine rises in the nucleus accumbens while serotonin drops in the cortex. Researchers provoke an aggressive episode at a specific time of day for 10 days, and then do nothing on the 11th day. What they observe is the same neurochemical change in the rodent's brain on the last day, despite the event not occurring. In effect, the rodent has been conditioned.
- **Hypothalamus stimulation.** Researchers discovered a locus of aggression in the hypothalamus by injecting a virus carrying a light-sensitive protein into the brain and then stimulating the

---

[6] This section summarizes information presented by Klaus Miczek, Tufts University.

protein. Afterward, the rodents can be triggered, by flashing a light, to attack both animate and inanimate objects. Miczek suggested that these findings could be explored further in the alcohol animal research.
- **Serotonin.** Numerous studies over the years have focused on serotonin and its effects on aggression and violence. Findings have been inconsistent because serotonin is a complex molecule. Serotonin neurons in the brainstem project to other parts of the brain in a segregated manner, so they can be individually turned off by inserting toxins in specific places. Additionally, only serotonin neurons that originate in subregions that also express dopamine receptions are important in aggressive behavior, indicating the system consists of parallel processes. Focusing on the relevant serotonin process has implications for research on the impact of alcohol.
- **GABA.** The GABA (γ-aminobutyric acid) receptor is the target of action for alcohol. Alcohol acts as a positive allosteric modulator to facilitate the action of GABA, an inhibitory neurotransmitter. Because of the biphasic effect of alcohol (i.e., pro-aggressive at low doses, sedative at high doses), it was originally thought that different mechanisms were involved. In the 1990s, researchers discovered that different genes encode subunits of the $GABA_A$ receptor, with the α-2 subunits related to pro-aggressive effects.
- **Glutamate.** The N-methyl-D-aspartate (NMDA) receptor is one of several glutamate receptors in the brain. It has a number of subunits, which can be targeted to alter psychotic episodes. In particular, the use of a specific Alzheimer drug, memantine, enhances aggression in individuals who do not show heightened aggression, but produces no effect on those who do. Glutamate and GABA act as a go-and-stop mechanism for serotonin, including serotonin subsystems responsible for heightened aggression.
- **Neuroendocrine factors.** There is some promising evidence that corticotropin-releasing factor receptor 1 (CRF_1) has a calming effect on mice with heightened aggression, possibly by mediating an aggression-related serotonin pathway.

Miczek closed by emphasizing the important role that the mouse model played in teasing apart the various pathways in the brain that result in aggressive behavior, particularly in relation to alcohol consumption, in a manner not possible in human research.

Alcohol Use and Intimate Partner Violence[7]

Kenneth Leonard remarked that the association between alcohol use and interpersonal violence has been observed in several cultures and contexts around the world, regardless of strictness of alcohol norms, level of violence, or other cultural overlays. This relationship has also been seen in multiple samples, including a nationally representative sample and criminal and clinical populations. It is an association of moderate strength and observed longitudinally, even when other factors related to aggression and conflict within relationships are controlled (Leonard and Senchak, 1996).

While there are effects of chronic use of alcohol, much of the aggression-related effects stem from the acute use of alcohol. Leonard noted that this can be studied in two ways: event-based research and experimental studies (largely in college students administered alcohol). Event-based research would include the examination of an event of partner violence, and a comparable event, such as a severe argument that did not result in violence. In a study Leonard conducted with his colleagues, couples were queried on alcohol consumption during conflicts involving verbal aggression, moderate physical aggression, and severe aggression. The husband's drinking was strongly associated with severe violence, while the wife's drinking was less clear (Leonard and Quigley, 1999). In another study, men and women described conflict episodes that did or did not involve violence in the months before alcohol abuse treatment. In the events that had physical conflict or violence, the husband's use of alcohol was higher (Murphy et al., 2005).

In experimental studies of alcohol and aggression, the aggression that is provoked is usually mild and not necessarily similar to violence seen in the community. Many of them include competitions that involve the "reward" of inflicting mild harm (e.g., a mild shock) on their opponent. Alcohol consumption tends to result in a more intense shock, an effect that is dose-dependent, while the placebo (i.e., no alcohol) has no effect (Bushman, 1997; Ito et al., 1996).

Other types of experimental studies look at alcohol use and aggressive verbal behavior. In the context of intimate partner violence, Leonard remarked, this makes sense as violence often emerges out of an ongoing verbal conflict. In one study, couples were invited to discuss a previously agreed upon topic of conflict, to establish a baseline. They were then separated for a period of time, and the husband was given alcohol. When they returned to discuss another conflict, the interaction was marked by very high levels of negativity on the part of both the husband and the wife, an effect not seen when a placebo was administered (Leonard and Roberts,

---

[7] This section summarizes information presented by Kenneth Leonard, Research Institute on Addictions.

1998). In a similar study, researchers also found that the association between alcohol and negativity was highest among those who also showed antisocial tendencies (Jacob et al., 2001).

Leonard proposed a cognitive disruption model to explain alcohol's impact on aggression. Intoxication leads to some level of cognitive impairment, to which people adapt by focusing on salient cues and missing subtle context. This theory suggests that alcohol should exacerbate overt emotions in certain settings—that is, a setting that evokes aggression would be heightened with alcohol, whereas a situation that evokes sadness would have low risk of aggression. Alcohol exacerbates a person's reaction to the most dominant cues and hides those that are peripheral and could be inhibiting (Parrott and Giancola, 2004). To the extent that mental illness is associated with negative affect and impaired self-control, Leonard postulated, alcohol might interact with psychopathology to create a high risk of violence. He showed one study that suggested a synergistic effect for substance use disorders and mental illness (Van Dorn et al., 2012).

Finally, successful treatment of alcohol use disorders results in a reduction of aggression. If sobriety levels are maintained, then both verbal and physical violence is reduced. If there is relapse, then the rate of violence increases again.

Evidence-Based Policies to Reduce Alcohol-Related Violence[8]

Alcohol creates a wide range of negative consequences that have implications in the public health policy realm. Toben Nelson observed that while several behaviors are risky, not all of them are public health issues because they do not result in population-level harm. Alcohol consumption, on the other hand, is a common social activity that is associated with several risks to the public as a whole. The risks associated with alcohol consumption increase as exposure increases. However, consumption of alcohol lies on a curve, with a larger number of the population at the lower consumption end, and a smaller number at the higher end. Thus, even though high consumption carries a greater risk to individuals, lower levels of consumption, which occur at greater frequency, pose a greater risk to the population as a whole. As epidemiologist Geoffrey Rose noted, "a large number of people exposed to a small risk may generate many more cases than a small number exposed to a high risk." The vast majority of health harms in a community arises from a moderate or lower level of risk.

This yields two approaches to harm reduction, Nelson noted: the high-risk approach that provides individual-level treatment, and a population-level

---

[8] This section summarizes information presented by Toben Nelson, University of Minnesota School of Public Health.

approach that aims to change behavior and the conditions that shape that behavior. Often, these two approaches are seen as oppositional, when they should be complementary. Nelson spoke of a theory developed by Alex Wagenaar and Cheryl Perry that looked at the relationship of high-risk individuals embedded within a community. While much research has focused on drinking and alcohol-related problems or individual risk factors that increase drinking behavior, Wagenaar and Perry considered that, within the community, there is a wide range of availability of alcohol. Problems of alcohol at the individual level are a function of the economic, legal, or physical availability of alcohol in those communities. This availability, in turn, is shaped by policies and norms around how alcohol is provided or restricted. Nelson and his colleagues examined the efficacy of some of these policies around the United States and created a list of the top 10:

1. Alcohol excise taxes (state)
2. State alcohol control systems (monopoly)
3. Bans on alcohol sales
4. Outlet density restrictions
5. Wholesale price restrictions
6. Retail price restrictions
7. Alcohol beverage control agencies that are present, functional, and adequately staffed
8. Dram shop liability laws
9. Hours of sale restrictions
10. Restrictions on alcohol consumption in public places and events

Regarding taxes, Nelson noted the evidence that price strategies are inversely related to violence: the higher the price of alcohol, the lower the rates of alcohol-related violence (Wagenaar et al., 2010). On alcohol retail density, studies show more violence and violent crime where there is greater density, and time-series data show increases in violence when alcohol outlets privatize and proliferate. Despite evidence for these types of programs being effective in reducing harm related to alcohol consumption, there has not been increased uptake of them, Nelson noted. Instead, policies judged to be less effective are on the rise in the United States.

Alcohol Policy: Challenges and Successes in Latin America[9]

In terms of the global burden of disease, alcohol has higher impacts in countries in Latin America than in the United States or Europe. In Brazil, an

---

[9] This section summarizes information presented by Ronaldo Laranjeira, Universidade Federal de São Paulo and National Institute on Alcohol and Drug Policy, Brazil.

unregulated alcohol market and close ties between the alcohol industry and politicians are challenges for the alcohol control policy landscape. There is little awareness among policymakers and little community involvement in alcohol policy, and there are few good examples of successful alcohol policies and programs within Brazil.

Ronaldo Laranjeira further described the unregulated market in Brazil: There is no licensing requirement to sell alcohol, resulting in nearly 1 alcohol outlet per 200 people. In addition, an estimated 30 percent of drivers on weekends are intoxicated, and there is little restriction on adolescent purchase of alcohol. The price of alcohol is inexpensive as well. Laranjeira noted that one can of beer costs 30 cents (by comparison, a liter of orange juice costs $3.50). Alcohol is also marketed heavily in Brazil. Laranjeira stated that normally, sale of alcohol in sports stadiums is forbidden by law. However, for the World Cup in 2014, lobbying from both the International Federation of Associated Football (FIFA) and the alcohol industry succeeded in changing that law.

Despite these and other challenges, Laranjeira shared an example of a successful program in the city of Diadema, in São Paulo state. Diadema has around 350,000 inhabitants, most of whom are low to middle class. In the 1990s, there was a high rate of homicides—102 per 100,000 people—with 50 percent occurring between 9 p.m. and 6 a.m. There was also a high rate of violence against women during that time, as well as a high incidence of gang activity and car crashes. In 2002, a municipal law was passed prohibiting the sale of alcohol between 11 p.m. and 6 a.m. The law was enforced, with local police verifying compliance every night. The first violation resulted in a warning, the second in a fine, and the third in a fine and the working permit license suspended. Despite the previously mentioned lack of licensing, enforcement on this law was active, and there was high approval among the community.

Ten years of homicide data were examined, from 1995 to 2005, including homicide data both before and after the law was enacted. The results showed that 528 lives were saved, with a 46 percent reduction in homicides. Additional years of data have reinforced this reduction in violence, with a homicide rate of less than 20 per 100,000 people in the past few years and a decrease in violence against women, as well (Duailibi et al., 2007). Laranjeira closed by noting that one important factor in the success of this program was the continued enforcement; success of program replications in other cities has decreased because of a failure to sustain the nightly police checks.

Discussion

In the ensuing discussion, speakers and workshop participants further explored some of the main themes raised, notably the importance of enforcement in setting policy and the role of the unregulated alcohol markets and the alcohol industry. Participants also discussed additional policy approaches, such as those that restrict alcohol use and firearms possession, and interventions that merge population-based and individual-focused perspectives.

REFERENCES

Andrés, R., and K. Hempstead. 2011. Gun control and suicide: The impact of state firearm regulations in the United States. *Health Policy* 101:95–103.

Bushman, B. J. 1997. Effects of alcohol on human aggression. Validity of proposed explanations. *Recent Developments in Alcoholism* 13:227–243.

Duailibi, S., W. Ponicki, J. Grube, I. Pinsky, R. Laranjeira, and M. Raw. 2007. The effect of restricting opening hours on alcohol-related violence. *American Journal of Public Health* 97(12):2276–2280.

Gunnell, D., M. Eddleston, M. Phillips, and F. Konradsen. 2007. The global distribution of fatal pesticide self-poisoning: Systematic review. *BMC Public Health* 7:357.

Ito, T. A., N. Miller, and V. E. Pollock. 1996. Alcohol and aggression: A meta-analysis on the moderating effects of inhibitory cues, triggering events, and self-focused attention. *Psychological Bulletin* 120(1):60–82.

Jacob, T., K. E. Leonard, and J. R. Haber. 2001. Family interactions of alcoholics as related to alcoholism. *Alcoholism: Clinical and Experimental Research* 25:834–843.

Leonard, K. E., and B. M. Quigley. 1999. Drinking and marital aggression in newlyweds: An event-based analysis of drinking and the occurrence of husband marital aggression. *Journal of Studies on Alcohol and Drugs* 60(4):537–545.

Leonard, K. E., and L. J. Roberts. 1998. The effects of alcohol on the marital interactions of aggressive and nonaggressive husbands and their wives. *Journal of Abnormal Psychology* 107(4):602–615.

Leonard, K. E., and M. Senchak. 1996. Prospective prediction of husband marital aggression within newlywed couples. *Journal of Abnormal Psychology* 105(3):369–380.

Miller, M., S. J. Lippmann, D. Azrael, and D. Hemenway. 2007. Household firearm ownership and rates of suicide across the 50 United States. *Journal of Trauma and Acute Care Surgery* 62(4):1029–1034.

Murphy, C. M., J. Winters, T. J. O'Farrell, W. Fals-Stewart, and M. Murphy. 2005. Alcohol consumption and intimate partner violence by alcoholic men: Comparing violent and nonviolent conflicts. *Psychology of Addictive Behaviors* 19(1):35–42.

Parrott, D. J., and P. R. Giancola. 2004. A further examination of the relation between trait anger and alcohol-related aggression: The role of anger control. *Alcoholism: Clinical and Experimental Research* 28(6):855–864.

Stevens, J. A., P. S. Corso, E. A. Finkelstein, and T. R. Miller. 2006. The costs of fatal and non-fatal falls among older adults. *Injury Prevention* 12(5):290–295.

Swanson, J. W., L. K. Frisman, A. G. Robertson, H. J. Lin, R. L. Trestman, D. A. Shelton, K. Parr, E. Rodis, A. Buchanan, and M. S. Swartz. 2013. Costs of criminal justice involvement among persons with serious mental illness in Connecticut. *Psychiatric Services* 64(7):630–637.

Van Dorn, R., J. Volavka, and N. Johnson. 2012. Mental disorder and violence: Is there a relationship beyond substance use? *Social Psychiatry and Psychiatric Epidemiology* 47(3):487–503.

Vigdor, E. R., and J. A. Mercy. 2006. Do laws restricting access to firearms by domestic violence offenders prevent intimate partner homicide? *Evaluation Review* 30(3):313–346.

Wagenaar, A. C., A. L. Toblet, and K. A. Komro. 2010. Effects of alcohol tax and price policies on morbidity and mortality: A systematic review. *American Journal of Public Health* 100(11):2270–2278.

Webster, D. W., J. S. Vernick, A. M. Zeoli, and J. A. Manganello. 2004. Association between youth-focused firearm laws and youth suicides. *JAMA* 292(5):594–601.

Wiebe, D. J. 2003. Homicide and suicide risks associated with firearms in the home: A national case-control study. *Annals of Emergency Medicine* 41(6):771–782.

5

Prevention, Intervention, and Treatment

Several systems, particularly mental health services and the justice system, play crucial roles in addressing mental illness and violence. If not established as supportive structures, they can cause harm and trauma and possibly increase the risk of violence. Speakers explored how these systems can protect and heal, by building positive environments and providing treatment and redress.

MENTAL HEALTH SERVICES AND VIOLENCE

Speakers discussed ways in which the provision of mental health services can both prevent and reduce violence. Access to care means appropriate treatment for people with mental illness, particularly for those who might seem disruptive to society and whose actions could result in the involvement of the justice system. Furthermore, early and universal mental health services, including those in schools, have implications for reduced violence prevalence across society by addressing risk factors directly. Speakers also discussed the role of policy and programs in expanding services and increasing access in the United States and Latin America.

Mental Health and Access to Services[1]

Stigma around mental health is often exacerbated by a perception of a higher risk of violence among those with mental illness. Colleen Barry cited

---

[1] This section summarizes information presented by Colleen Barry, Johns Hopkins Bloomberg School of Public Health.

a study that found 46 percent of those surveyed believe that people with serious mental illness are much more dangerous than those without; 29 percent were willing to work closely with someone with a mental illness, and 33 percent were willing to have a neighbor with a mental illness. These perceptions are also affected by whether the respondents had experience, either directly or through a family member or close friend, with mental illness. This context, Barry argued, is important for considering the connection between public attitudes and broader support for mental health services.

Many people experience mental illness, and seeking care is common; one in five seeks care yearly, and one in three over the lifetime. Broadly speaking, she asserted, treatment history or diagnosis is not a specific or useful predictor of violence. Most people with mental illness do not commit acts of violence, and most violent acts are not committed by people with a diagnosis of mental disorder. Less than 2 percent of the population meets the diagnostic criteria for severe and persistent mental illness, and it is a subgroup of those—adults with conduct disorders in childhood—that has the strongest association with violence. But even among that subgroup, the majority is not violent but instead is more likely to be victims of violence.

Given this background, Barry asked, can access to services impact violence? She described two types of services most often discussed: broad institutionalized care and universal screening. On the first, she observed that there is no clear association between institutionalized care and patterns of violence among people with severe and persistent mental illness. Additionally, there are several civil rights challenges with institutionalization and its history of practice. On universal screening, she pointed out there is both low specificity for screening instruments and a lack of capacity in the system for the additional individuals who might be identified in screening. She concluded that broad approaches are not likely to be effective in reducing violence related to severe mental health disorders.

There is a role, she noted, for targeted interventions that improve access and treatment for adolescents with conduct disorders, particularly interventions that address co-occurring mental health and substance use disorders or that are oriented toward suicide prevention. Yet, many of them have not been well implemented. She emphasized, however, that there are reasons beyond violence to improve behavioral health systems in the United States, such as dealing with undertreatment and inappropriate treatment, quality of care, and even measuring and tracking quality. This has implications for payment and insurance, particularly in the context of performance-based metrics. In contrast to the overall health care system, Medicaid plays a much larger role in covering the costs of care and treatment, while private insurance is limited. Even within insurance schemes, historically, mental health services have been underprovisioned and underfunded. However, people with severe mental illnesses are uninsured at a much higher rate than people with no mental diagnosis.

The Paul Wellstone and Pete Domenici Mental Health Parity and Addiction Equity Act, enacted in 2008, was intended to equalize coverage for mental health and substance use services, as comparable to other health services within an insurance program, including not only coinsurance, but deductibles and copayments, as well. It also required that insurance program designs, including elements such as prior authorization and provider networks, had to be equal. Its impact is significant, especially in providing out-of-pocket financial protection.

The Patient Protection and Affordable Care Act of 2010, designed to expand access to and affordability of all health care services, has also resulted in increased coverage of mental health services. Barry explained that this increase is due to an expansion of public programs, reform and redesign of insurance markets, and delivery system and payment reform. While the state health insurance exchanges account for some of the expansion, the bulk of it is a result of Medicaid expansion, particularly the new Medicaid Health Home option, which allows for different types of services that have not been traditionally financed but are important for coordinating care.

The new health care provisions also have implications for criminal justice. People in prisons have the option to enroll in or maintain Medicaid, which provides continuity of coverage. For those on antipsychotics, for example, this means continued medication access and could result in lowered recidivism. Barry closed with a reflection about stigma and mental health, citing a recent study of her own in which, when presented with information about the recovery and treatment of people with mental illness, survey respondents responded more favorably when asked if they would be willing to work closely with or live next to a person with mental illness. Such vignettes, she observed, could dramatically alter public perception on mental illness and improve mental health services and access.

Role of School Mental Health in Mental Health Promotion and Violence Prevention[2]

School mental health was defined by Sharon Stephan as a partnership between schools and community health and behavioral health organizations, guided by youth and families. While it includes students in special education, its scope is all students and a full array of services from universal prevention to tertiary care. Of the roughly 96,000 public schools in the United States, approximately 40 percent of them indicated that mental

---

[2] This section summarizes information presented by Sharon Stephan, University of Maryland.

health services were provided by a combination of school employees and community employees. An additional 32 percent indicated services were only provided by school staff, and another 28 percent by outside partners.

The community partnership offers schools the ability to provide a broad continuum of care beyond what school staff provides. Community partners also reduce necessary and expensive services, such as emergency room visits, by facilitating pathways, providing preventive care, and assisting with transition from inpatient psychiatric care back to schools. It is important to note, however, that community partners are building on the school's existing platform and supplanting staff.

Mental health service provision in schools is based on a few principles:

- Healthy students make better learners, and students who succeed in school are more likely to be healthy.
- Adult mental health has its roots in childhood experiences and mental health, and early treatment yields better prognosis in adulthood.
- About one in five children will experience mild mental health impairment, and one in 10 will experience severe impairment. Many of them do not receive the care they need outside of school (McKay et al., 2005), so schools serve as a de facto mental health system for children.
- Addressing mental health in school versus in the community means less time lost from school or work for students and their parents, respectively.

Stephan stated that promising evidence suggests that there are benefits to in-school mental health services. Around social and emotional learning and universal mental health promotion, there are improvements in student social competency and behavioral and emotional functioning. Additionally, improvements are seen in academic indicators, such as grades, test scores, attendance, and teacher retention. There is also evidence of cost savings to schools and communities.

In looking at violence, Stephan remarked that youth are exposed to violence in a variety of settings, including school and home, and more than 60 percent of them report lifetime exposure to traumatic events (McLaughlin et al., 2013). One in five youth report being physically assaulted by peers; a similar proportion report emotional violence by peers, as well. The school is a common setting for physical intimidation, assault, and emotional violence, with more than half of all incidents occurring in school (Turner et al., 2011). During the 2009 school year, 1 in 10 schools reported a serious violent incident that required the presence of criminal law enforcement (Robers et al., 2012). Moreover, 16 percent of students report carrying a firearm to school, and 6 percent of students report missing school because of safety concerns (CDC, 2008). This violence has repercussions for educational attainment. For example, in a study in Baltimore, Maryland, increasing violence was associated with reduced reading achievement in elementary school students, while increasing perception of safety was associated with higher achievement (Milam et al., 2010).

A public health approach to violence prevention in schools would have multiple intervention points, including the student, the classroom, the school, and the community. In addition, evidence-based health interventions focus more broadly on safety, rather than on just security, as the research suggests that measures such as security cameras and guards are not effective. The interventions with evidence of success include environmental design, teaching students to be peer mediators, and multifamily group intervention.

Stephan presented further information on one particular intervention, Positive Behavioral Intervention and Supports (PBIS), which is a schoolwide framework targeting school climate. PBIS is currently in about 20,000 schools. Some evidence suggests that PBIS improves perception of safety and reduces aggressive behavior. Elements of the intervention include adapting the environment through natural surveillance, access management (e.g., better signage), physical maintenance, visibility maximization, and order maintenance.

Mental Health in Latin America and the Caribbean[3]

The Global Burden of Disease shows depression as the second largest cause of disability globally. In Latin America and the Caribbean (LAC), 14 percent of disability-adjusted life years (DALYs) and 35 percent of years lost to disability (YLDs) are related to mental health and neurological disorders. Treatment gaps for mental disorders, such as anxiety, schizophrenia, depression, and alcohol use disorder, in LAC are also higher than global rates (Kohn et al., 2004).

Globally, there is also an insufficiency of mental health resources: the world median percentage of the public health budget dedicated to mental health is less than 3 percent. In LAC, the majority of countries allocate between 1 and 5 percent of the public budget to mental health, with a small number of countries having no allocation whatsoever. Of the monies dedicated to mental health, 88 percent goes to mental hospitals, which leaves only 12 percent (of the less than 5 percent) for community-based services. Dévora Kestel remarked that in LAC, there are on average 2 psychiatrists,

---

[3] This section summarizes information presented by Dévora Kestel, Pan American Health Organization.

4 psychologists, and 1 social worker per 100,000 people. Additionally, she noted that the majority of these personnel work in psychiatric hospitals or psychiatric units in hospitals; across LAC, less than 40 percent of them work in ambulatory care. Nonpersonnel resources, in particular beds, are also concentrated in the hospitals, with very little community housing. Kestel also commented on the variation and quality of mental health policy; most policies are outdated and would not meet internationally agreed upon standards.

The Pan American Health Organization's work in the region is focused on two aspects: leadership and governance, and mental health and social care services. Greater investment in both aspects is needed, Kestel felt, because the mental health burden in LAC cannot be addressed solely by mental health professionals, but should be integrated with primary care and community care. And importantly, without a more comprehensive and better funded approach to mental health, there cannot be a system to address violence and care for victims and perpetrators.

Discussion

Several themes raised by the speakers were further explored by audience participants following the presentations. In the absence of a robust community mental health system, and with limited capacity of mental health professionals, prisons in the United States have served the role of mental health care providers—a situation that participants felt was not necessarily one to emulate in other parts of the world. In particular, as children leave school for various mental health or violence issues, many of them end up in prison. Michael Phillips of the Shanghai Mental Health Center noted that in China the transition of mental health care from involuntary commitment to voluntary has resulted in more people with mental illness ending up in prison. He commented that training community health workers in mental health could be one way to address the personnel shortage, while others noted that integrating mental health and general health could address issues in both domains.

INTERFACE WITH THE JUSTICE COMMUNITY AND OPPORTUNITIES FOR INTERVENTION

Gaps in community mental health care have resulted in an increased role for the criminal justice system in addressing mental health needs. At the same time, a disproportionate number of people with mental illness are incarcerated, and the correctional system has an obligation to meet their psychiatric needs. Speakers discussed the ways in which the justice system can serve those needs, as well as how it can be a supportive environment rather than a punitive one.

Encounters with the Justice Community and Opportunities for Intervention[4]

Madelon Baranoski described early mental health linkages to the justice system, noting that, historically, those who could not afford private care often ended up in prisons. In a time when there were no effective treatments for severe mental illness, reformers worked to move people to other facilities where, though they were still isolated from the general public, they would be treated more fairly. These facilities became modern-day asylums, and care deteriorated. With the advent of treatment options for severe mental illness, it was no longer considered humane to isolate people without due process. The U.S. Supreme Court in 1966 declared that dangerousness was a prerequisite for involuntary commitment, and the process of deinstitutionalization began.

However, with the transition of people with severe mental illness from institutions to the community, there was no additional provision for care or treatment. And while Baranoski cautioned that not everyone with a mental illness is violent, a number of them end up in prison for what she termed "nuisance crimes," such as breach of peace. Baronski went on to note that while the number of people with mental illness in prison is increasing, the increase is not because of violence, but rather because life is becoming more destabilized. Poverty, low education, limited housing and resources, and discrimination contribute to the increased number of people with mental illness in prison. In addition, the public misperception that people with mental illness are more dangerous results in the justice system taking control where it seems the mental health system has failed. Jails and prisons, Baranoski asserted, should be the last step. The interface begins with policing, moves to the courts, and if all else fails, ends up in prison. Box 5-1 describes a few of the issues that arise in this process.

Public Safety and Mental Health[5]

Police play an important and complex role in community mental health services, but, as Sheldon Greenberg noted, there are many areas in need of improvement. Some areas are easier and simpler to address, such as terminology. For example, the Association of Public-Safety Communications Officials International (APCO) uses the code "10-96," which translates to "mental subject," rather than "person with mental illness." This change, he asserted, is a simple one to make, but is still an important one.

---

[4] This section summarizes information presented by Madelon Baranoski, Yale University.

[5] This section summarizes information presented by Sheldon Greenberg, Johns Hopkins University School of Education.

> **BOX 5-1**
> **Issues Across the Criminal Justice System**
>
> **Law Enforcement:** Excessive force, involuntary treatment, symptom management without arrest, interviewing, reliability of victims' reports, protection of public, risk of injury to police, civil rights, local customs, cost, and training.
>
> **The Courts:** Civil rights, societal values, equal protection, competency to proceed, competency to be a witness, competency to accept a plea, appropriate punishment, protection of public, risk of recidivism, capacity to serve probation, access to alternatives, cost, and training.
>
> **Department of Correction:** Constitutional right to treatment, constitutional right to refuse treatment, forced medication, overcrowding, definition of mental illness, lack of resources, safety, access to parole, community reintegration, cost, and training.

He further observed that police officers think that their work is misunderstood by researchers and other social service providers. For example, about 70 percent of police work does not involve law enforcement, and much of a police officer's interaction with the public is not recorded. Many police officers would like to do more to serve people with mental illness, but barriers of time and resources stand in the way (Cooper et al., 2004).

The justice system in the United States is one of the most fragmented professional systems in the country, Greenberg remarked. There are about 18,000 state and local law enforcement agencies in the United States; however, if a department has fewer than 10 officers, it is not required to report within the federal system. Across the world, police agencies are sometimes military or quasi-military operations or they fall under the purview of a national police system. Similarly, the court system is fragmented, and sound data do not exist on numbers because many courts are temporary. Incarceration is not well integrated either: prisons, jails, and lockups are distinct places and fall under different jurisdictions, police departments, sheriff departments, departments of corrections, county jails, and state and federal penitentiaries.

In addition to the fragmentation, Greenberg observed that the conversation around deinstitutionalization and community-based services occurred before the majority of today's police departments were in service, and there is still miscommunication around mental health issues. Additionally, policing is primarily a reactive profession—that is, police officers respond to calls and attempt to resolve them on the spot. Greenberg stated that, on average, an officer has approximately 2.5 seconds to react appropriately when deciding if the situation calls for the use of lethal or nonlethal force. However, police officers receive minimal training on mental health—only an average of 2.5 hours, most of which is focused on process and not purpose or ideology. This is within the context of 16 to 24 weeks of academy training, with an additional 8 to 12 weeks of field training. Between minimal training and limited personnel, police face several challenges in providing appropriate services to people with mental illness, several of which are outlined in Box 5-2.

Greenberg raised several additional concerns at the intersection of law enforcement and mental health. There are an estimated 1.2 million people with mental illness currently incarcerated, but it is not clear how many have already been sentenced and how many are in jail awaiting trial. Many of these individuals face a significant amount of bias. Furthermore, there is miscommunication and distrust between the police and the community, which could be improved with some bidirectional learning. He gave the example of working with the National Association for the Deaf to reduce killings of deaf people that occurred at traffic stops because of

---

BOX 5-2
What Police Patrol Officers Want Mental Health Practitioners to Know

Sample of comments:

- I function alone.
- I am the only officer on duty this shift.
- My immediate focus is on safety. I need to know about the crisis at hand, who is hurt or in danger, the environment, and access to weapons. Talk about mental illness, what happened in the past, and everything else will occur later.
- The closest hospital to my beat is 25 miles away.
- People with mental illness and their families don't know what to expect when I arrive.
- At 3:30 a.m. on a Sunday, I don't have access to mental health workers or county attorneys . . . if I get hold of them they don't want to come out.
- The family calls and wants help . . . then when I explain what I can or have to do, they turn on me. It's tough. I understand. They want intervention without consequence. They want help I'm not able to give.
- You need to know how we approach potentially life-threatening situations.
- We're criticized for using force. We follow a use-of-force continuum. We can't take chances. It is better to be judged by 12 than carried by 6.

misunderstanding. Police were better trained, but it was not until there was outreach in the deaf community that the shootings were reduced.

Greenberg closed by noting that rather than focusing on top-level goals, such as policy, procedure, or funding, interventions primarily should focus on point of entry. He noted two specific groups that could benefit from interventions focused on the point of entry: emergency dispatchers, who gather and disseminate information and thereby create the foundation for potential encounters, and the police, who interact with the affected family or the environment in a direct way. Better training and support for emergency dispatchers and police is particularly crucial.

Education and Treatment as Alternatives for Incarceration[6]

Ray Kotwicki spoke about an intervention used successfully at Emory University. It is a 4-year program for medical students to help people identify patients who have symptoms of mental illness, such as impulsivity and para-suicidality, in primary care clinics and other places. The intervention is designed to divert such people away from the penal justice system and toward treatment. Kotwicki noted that once people agree to treatment, there need to be good treatment options. Skyland Trail, his community treatment facility in Atlanta, Georgia, is one such innovative center.

Health professionals tend to view the mental health field with negativity, argued Kotwicki, and medical students typically are not attracted to psychiatry. This is partially because of misperceptions around mental illness and treatment, as well as a lack of understanding of the biological basis of mental illness. In addition, people who do psychiatry clerkships in facilities where containment, not recovery, is the goal tend to have a less positive experience in working with people with mental illness. Thus, part of the work at Skyland Trail is also educational, to engage health professionals in a more positive way when addressing mental health.

Skyland Trail also incorporates educational programs for law enforcement. Kotwicki and his colleagues studied the impact of a 2-day training for police officers involving mental health professionals, including doctors and nurses. They saw a robust, statistically significant improvement in attitudes and knowledge about how to manage situations involving people with symptoms of mental illness. This finding tracks with other research, in which exposure to an individual with mental illness is one of the best ways to reduce personal stigma.

The same paradigm shift for engaging professionals also applies to treatment for patients' recovery. Periodic measurement of indicators associated with violence, such as psychosis and impulsivity, and indicators related

---

[6] This section summarizes information presented by Ray Kotwicki, Skyland Trail.

to social relationships and immediate environment, can shed light on how engagement of professionals can positively impact recovery. Using pre- and post-test outcome assessments of these indicators, Skyland Trail has shown statistically significant improvement in people who underwent the program, not just in symptomology but in managing relationships and quality of life to reduce violent behavior. Kotwicki concluded his presentation by emphasizing the importance of access: proper treatment can yield great benefits, but only if people can be directed toward and reach such programs.

Therapeutic Jurisprudence[7]

Therapeutic jurisprudence is a healing approach to the law, with the intention of "rehabilitation, compliance with the law, and helping victims to cope with the impact of crime on their lives," David Wexler stated. He explained that therapeutic jurisprudence is best known in special problem-solving or solution-focused courts, such as drug treatment court, mental health court, and domestic violence court. The law has an effect on well-being. This effect has been largely ignored in administration of the law, but Wexler argued that it should be studied and factored into law reform. The Hague Institute for Innovation of Law is exploring options to maintain therapeutic jurisprudence, particularly in criminal law and juvenile justice. It is an interdisciplinary approach that involves psychology, criminology, and social work, as well as working with offenders and victims.

While it has mostly been used in specialized courts, the therapeutic jurisprudence approach has broader implications for those who fail to meet the qualifications of those special courts. Attempts to expand the special courts often encounter budget obstacles, so a second option is to apply the skills and insights elsewhere in the criminal justice system, in which people with mental illness or drug or alcohol problems might find themselves. Wexler suggested that there are several elements that could be incorporated with the wider system, such as early diversion, bail hearings, plea negotiations, judicial settlement conferences, non-incarcerative sentences, and conditional release. Wexler noted that his project also examines police interrogation and newer, more humanistic methods of investigative interviewing, even before a person's entry into the court system. In this way, he remarked, the project looks at both the law in action and the roles of legal actors, including judges, lawyers, and therapists.

In exploring how such elements might be included in criminal justice, Wexler noted that he and his colleagues examined which practices are in place already, which are not, why they are not, and how they could be

---

[7] This section summarizes information presented by David Wexler, International Network of Therapeutic Jurisprudence.

maximized. They also examined what kind of training would be required for legal actors to incorporate therapeutic jurisprudence insights. It is also important, he explained, to note which existing structures allow for adaptability to new processes, and which legal structures might need to be reformed. He gave the example of probation, which is traditionally handed down unilaterally by a judge. Instead, the literature indicates that soliciting offender input, such as asking him or her to personally justify a probationary sentence and conditions, enhances offender compliance and a sense of fair treatment.

At its heart, Wexler remarked, therapeutic jurisprudence is multidisciplinary and draws from insights of different realms. He concluded by citing important research areas: relapse prevention planning, reasoning and rehabilitation, desistance from crime, treatment adherence, behavioral contracting, active listening, and restorative justice.

Behavioral Health Care in Correctional Facilities[8]

Patrick Fox described the shift of population, cost, and burden from community-based and state-hospital-based mental health systems to the correctional system as trans-institutionalization. Since the mid-1970s, the prison population has steadily increased. Currently, there are approximately 2.5 million individuals incarcerated, with another 4.2 million on parole or probation—representing 2.9 percent of the population. The vast majority of those entering the criminal justice system, particularly those with behavioral health disorders, are not being arrested for violent crimes. Yet, among people with behavioral health disorders, there is a 40 percent lifetime prevalence of incarceration. Additionally, there are huge racial disparities, with African American and Hispanic individuals being grossly overrepresented. Fox emphasized that these racial disparities pervade the entire criminal justice system, from death penalty cases to insanity pleas, and even probation and parole decisions (though there is no correlation between the race of the arresting officer and these disproportionate incarceration rates of people of color). The increase in prison populations also trends with a commensurate increase in substance use arrests.

People with behavioral health disorders are also overrepresented in the criminal justice system, especially as mental institutions close. Currently, about half of those within the correctional system experience some form of mental illness. This is a problem because the focus of psychiatric hospitals is on the restoration of health and treatment, whereas correctional facilities are intended to contain and punish. Fox further discussed the differences between mental health facilities and prisons:

---

[8] This section summarizes information presented by Patrick Fox, University of Colorado.

- **Treatment versus security.** 90 percent of staff at a state psychiatric hospital are mental health professionals or support staff, and security is an ancillary service. In a prison or jail, 90 percent of staff are correctional officers, with security equipment, while therapy is a secondary consideration.
- **Crisis intervention.** When there is a behavioral health emergency, correctional officers are usually first responders in a correctional facility. However, mental health staff who manage such events in psychiatric hospitals have a greater understanding of trauma-informed care and recovery.
- **Standards.** The Joint Commission and the Centers for Medicare & Medicaid Services serve as crediting bodies for hospitals, whereas the American Correctional Association and the National Commission on Correctional Health Care work on the correctional side.
- **Discharge.** Release from a mental health facility is based on recovery, whereas release from prison is conditioned on resolving the criminal offense.

Fox stated that within correctional facilities, prisoners have a right to treatment, as mandated by several court rulings. *Ruiz v. Estelle* in 1980 laid down six criteria for mental health services:

1. Systematic screening and evaluation
2. Treatment that is not just close observation or seclusion
3. Trained mental health professionals
4. Confidential and complete medical records (separate from the custody record)
5. Safeguards governing the use of psychotropic medications
6. A suicide prevention program

Additional laws, such as the Americans with Disabilities Act (ADA), have also served to improve quality of care. Entities such as the National Commission on Correctional Health Care and the much older American Correctional Association provide standards for 90 percent of jails and prisons in the United States. Because of these laws and standards, mental health treatment has improved. A 2000 report indicated that 95 percent of adult correctional facilities comply with screening requirements, but other quality measures are lower (Beck and Maruschak, 2001).

Mental health treatment varies greatly between jails and prisons because of differences in funding and standards at the local, state, and federal levels. How a community chooses to allocate funds (that could go toward other systems) can constrain or expand treatment services. In particular, because incarceration is still seen as a punishment, there is resistance to funding and provision of mental health services in jails.

When treatment is available, Fox said, the goal is shifting from preventing poor outcomes to a more proactive approach of developing independent living and social skills. Therapy is now focused on improving mood and functioning, modifying behavior, and developing vocational skills for future employment. Different treatment modalities exist, including group therapy, though their implementation is not always of the highest standard. Standards around the use of medication have also been altered: there is a much narrower mandate for the use of medications, and in all cases except emergencies, informed consent must be obtained. When consent cannot be obtained, there must be a clear rationale for the use of medication, as well as documentation of any side effects.

Another crucial mental health measure is suicide prevention. Thus, current standards require screening and assessment for suicide risk in correctional facilities. Fox noted that suicide is the second leading cause of death in jails and the third leading cause of death in prisons. Half of completed suicides occur within the first week of incarceration. Among the interventions to reduce suicide are reducing means (e.g., no fixtures in cells, cameras, and monitoring for substance withdrawal), reducing distress by allowing contact with family members, and monitoring changes in mood around any court dates.

Administrative segregation, or solitary confinement, is another issue in correctional facilities. Fox referred to it as a dehumanizing environment with pronounced psychological effects. Persons with mental illness are overrepresented in administrative segregation, and there is evidence that it exacerbates pre-existing mental conditions (Metzner, 2002). Fox suggested that the externalizing behaviors of someone with mental illness could be seen as disruptive behavior within a correctional facility and might result in the use of administrative segregation. The increased decompensation and limited access to mental health professionals could result in prolonged confinement, as well.

Despite the challenges and limitations of addressing mental health in the current incarceration system, there are shifts occurring. Fox shared the restorative justice model, an approach that focuses on the needs of the victim and the offender, the prevention of recidivism, and the duty of the community to maintain peace and restore order. Restorative justice programs help individuals take inventory and accountability of actions and understand where the origins of their criminogenic behavior reside. Correctional facilities with these programs would have special management units and treatment facilities for those with mental illness. And perhaps most important are offender re-entry programs, particularly programs that include outreach by community mental health professionals, that prepare individuals with mental illness to successfully reintegrate into communities.

REFERENCES

Beck, A. J., and L. M. Maruschak. 2001. *Mental health treatment in state prisons, 2000*. Bureau of Justice Statistics Special Report. Washington, DC: U.S. Department of Justice.

CDC (Centers for Disease Control and Prevention). 2008. *Youth risk behavior survey data*. www.cdc.gov/yrbs (accessed November 30, 2017).

Cooper, V. G., A. M. Mclearen, and P. A. Zapf. 2004. Dispositional decisions with the mentally ill: Police perceptions and characteristics. *Police Quarterly* 7(3):295–310.

Kohn, R., S. Saxena, I. Levav, and B. Saraceno. 2004. The treatment gap in mental health care. *Bulletin of the World Health Organization* 82(11):858–866.

McKay, M. M., C. J. Lynn, and W. M. Bannon. 2005. Understanding inner city child mental health need and trauma exposure: Implications for preparing urban service providers. *American Journal of Orthopsychiatry* 75(2):201–210.

McLaughlin, K. A., K. C. Koenen, E. D. Hill, M. Petukhova, N. A. Sampson, A. M. Zaslavsky, and R. C. Kessler. 2013. Trauma exposure and posttraumatic stress disorder in a national sample of adolescents. *Journal of the American Academy of Child & Adolescent Psychiatry* 52(8):815–830.

Metzner, J. L. 2002. Class action litigation in correctional psychiatry. *Journal of the American Academy of Psychiatry and the Law* 30(1):19–29.

Milam, A. J., C. D. M. Furr-Holden, and P. J. Leaf. 2010. Perceived school and neighborhood safety, neighborhood violence, and academic achievement in urban school children. *Urban Review* 42(5):458–467.

Robers, S., J. Kemp, J. Truman, and T. D. Snyder. 2012. *Indicators of school crime and safety: 2011*. Washington, DC: National Center for Education Statistics, U.S. Department of Education and Bureau of Justice Statistics, Office of Justice Programs, U.S. Department of Justice. http://nces.ed.gov/pubs2012/2012002.pdf (accessed November 30, 2017).

Turner, H. A., D. Finkelhor, S. L. Hamby, A. Shattuck, and R. K. Ormrod. 2011. Specifying type and location of peer victimization in a national sample of children and youth. *Journal of Youth and Adolescence* 40(8):1052–1067.

6

Assembling the Pieces and Integrating Elements

Throughout the workshop, participants shared a myriad of experiences, evidence, and practice in multiple domains related to mental health and violence prevention. In the last panel of the workshop, speakers and participants communicated knowledge and best practices on inexpensive and more nimble program evaluation. They also discussed final thoughts and raised additional questions on advancing the science and practice.

EVALUATION OF PROGRAMS FOR VIOLENCE PREVENTION AND MENTAL HEALTH PROMOTION[1]

A number of traditional and alternative evaluation designs can be used to assess the efficacy of violence prevention programs, by addressing important questions such as could a program work under optimal conditions? Does a program work under realistic conditions? And how does a program work, and can it be improved? Hendricks Brown described a 2009 National Research Council and Institute of Medicine report that laid out these three stages of evaluation, starting with efficacy and effectiveness studies and leading to implementation and dissemination studies (NRC and IOM, 2009). The former two address whether a program achieves the desired outcomes, and the latter deal with adoption, sustainability, and scaling up, and require different evaluation models.

---

[1] This section summarizes information presented by Hendricks Brown, Northwestern University.

Issues of evaluation are value-laden, he remarked, not just from a scientific perspective, but also a community perspective. Of note, there is a history of abuse in research, particularly in communities of color. There are also issues of cost, some of which disproportionately burden nongovernmental organizations that work with people of color. He further explained that these issues need to be confronted upfront because they are relevant to whether an evaluation can be carried out. He cautioned, though, that if a program is to be considered evidence based or evidence informed, it should have information to that end, at least under some set of circumstances. At a minimum, certain indicators could be measured, such as program fidelity and participation. Furthermore, Brown said the gold standard for evaluation is the randomized controlled trial (RCT) because it is designed to eliminate as many biases as possible. He noted that while sound evaluation evidence can be obtained from an RCT, sometimes it is unethical or impractical to conduct one.

Because violence is a relatively low-frequency event, large studies are needed to observe the effect sizes that indicate program success. He described the example of looking at completed suicide in youth. Because the youth suicide rate is small, it is estimated that a study would require at least 1 million person-years of risk, which would mean following 1 million youth for 1 year or 100,000 youth for 10 years; it would require intense labor input to follow up with so many individuals. Such large studies are expensive. Thus, he considered other options to enrolling large numbers of people in trials. The first is to look at an intermediary outcome; for example, assessing suicide attempts versus completed suicide, because attempts occur at a higher frequency than completed suicides. The second is to combine data across trials and synthesize findings. A third approach is to use a less expensive evaluation design, such as using administrative records to screen and identify individuals over a long period of time. The Positive Parenting Program, or Triple P, a family support program to prevent behavioral and emotional problems in children, used such an approach. In the United States, the National Death Index and the National Violent Death Reporting System are other sources of data.

Additionally, he described a method he called "roll-out design," sometimes referred to as "dynamic wait list design" and "stepped wedge trial design," in which groups are randomized to treatment and control groups as the program is rolled out. It has the added benefit of allowing an examination of the implementation strategy. He gave an example of one such program, which used a suicide gatekeeper program called Question, Persuade, and Refer (QPR) in a school district. The program was rolled out to randomly assigned schools, with new schools added each quarter. The outcome, school referrals for suicide, was measured before and after the schools were enrolled. By using a rolling method of enrollment, the first year and the first three quarters of the second year always maintained a control group (i.e., un-enrolled) for comparison. One of the advantages of this methodology is that, when the whole community has agreed to the intervention, there is still a process for incorporating everyone. Because all the schools received the intervention, there was no delay or associated costs. At the same time, there was a benefit to the schools that received the intervention first because often school districts are eager to implement a program sooner rather than later. However, those who receive the intervention later have the advantage of more efficient implementation. Finally, an important benefit of roll-out design is that evaluation is built into implementation—meaning that cost issues around evaluation may be averted and that accountability is naturally integrated with the process.

Once a program has been deemed effective, the final step in evaluation is making a program work. Brown noted that there are two areas for this step. On the research side, implementation science gathers generalized knowledge of program design; while on the practice side, quality improvement is an ongoing local evaluation. He shared the RE-AIM perspective for ensuring program success:

- Reach: the percentage of the community that receives the program
- Effectiveness: does the program have benefit?
- Adoption: bring into host organizations and service-delivery systems
- Implementation with fidelity
- Maintenance

Brown further noted that these measurable elements determine whether the implementation will be successful.

In the discussion following the presentation, participants queried Brown regarding issues of sustainability, such as funding evaluations and ensuring continuity and consistency as personnel change at program sites. Participants discussed requiring a measure of evaluation in grant proposals and the importance of building partnerships with the entire community. They also considered alternate methods of gathering data for evaluation, such as practice-based evidence and ongoing data collection in mobile health (mHealth) programs, that could integrate with traditional methods.

REFLECTIONS AND THE WAY FORWARD

The workshop closed by synthesizing the discussions over the 2 days, with participants offering reactions and thoughts on the topics presented. They spoke from multiple perspectives, reflecting the diversity of opinions and practices present at the workshop.

Mental Health Services[2]

Colleen Barry recalled Thomas Insel's remarks that untreated mental illness and alcohol and substance use disorders are associated with violence, and there is a role for mental health services and policies. She noted that there is also a role for understanding evidence; from a program perspective, dissemination is a critical piece in seeing translation of evidence into practice. Despite several rigorous studies demonstrating evidence of certain practices, there has been very little uptake of these programs. She also said that, in regard to evaluation, there is a role for examining unintended consequences of policies.

One way to implement and disseminate services and policies would be to create a financial incentive, such as an appropriately applied pay-for-performance model. She gave the example of an accountable care organization in Massachusetts with 64 different performance measures. Because only one measure was related to the population of individuals with mental health and substance use disorders, there was little change in regard to that system of care. She closed by noting that sustainability is critical, and financing and insurance changes can be instrumental as well.

Mental Health and Justice[3]

Sheldon Greenberg reflected on the knowledge gap between the mental health field and the justice system. He noted that while mental illness plays a significant role in justice, it is not on the radar of the politically driven system. Within all disciplines of the mental health field, the end goal is the same: better quality of service and support for people with mental illness. So what, he queried, is the formula for achieving this goal, and how can practitioners, researchers, and advocates develop it? He envisioned this formula to be cross-cutting, with different stakeholders having the ability to refine it for their own practices.

He echoed Barry's comments about disseminating research, also noting that along the translation pathway, barriers exist that inhibit frontline professionals from accessing research around what works. Other types of research are of interest as well. When a patient first comes in contact with the system, what happens to the information that is initially provided? How does that impact interventions? Research on fear was also of interest to Greenberg, particularly people's fear of what will occur after the initial contact that might inhibit them from being honest. Knowing more about this

---

[2] This section summarizes information presented by Colleen Barry, Johns Hopkins Bloomberg School of Public Health.
[3] This section summarizes information presented Sheldon Greenberg, Johns Hopkins University School of Education.

fear could assist in developing more trust with professionals and countering misinformation in the media and the general public.

He closed by asserting that cross-disciplinary collaboration for policy, coupled with mandates for providing better education and training in all fields, could build an institutional culture of understanding across all disciplines. In parallel to this work in professional fields, people with mental illness and their families, he argued, should be better equipped to engage the system at any point of contact.

Culture and Construction of Mental Health[4]

Janis Jenkins reiterated her earlier comment that empirical research demonstrates the central place of culture in nearly every aspect of mental illness. Thus, the ecological model of risk and protective factors could be enhanced by integrating culture across different domains, such as the individual and his or her relationship to community and society. Understanding the role of culture will require a deeper, broader understanding and could include research, such as ethnography of people and their encounters with violence as both victims and perpetrators. In particular, more information is needed about adolescents and their view of the cultural legitimacy of their frustration, anger, and violence, as well as ethnographic research on the culture of law enforcement and cultural assumptions, toward the goal of more reciprocal engagement.

For effective community intervention programs, Jenkins emphasized a need to account for the cultural aspects of the relationship between mental illness and violence, particularly in incorporating the perspective and expertise of people with mental illness, and to acknowledge the limitations of psychopharmacology as treatment. She also considered the importance of the school setting in teaching what constitutes a culture of violence. Finally, she closed by challenging the culture of scarcity as an excuse for failing to adequately support mental health programs.

Global Perspectives of Mental Health[5]

Dévora Kestel challenged the notion that further research on mental illness is needed, stating that she wished it were possible to implement even one-third of what is known. Instead, research on services that are intervention- and action-oriented is more important for those who want

---

[4] This section summarizes information presented by Janis Jenkins, University of California, San Diego.

[5] This section summarizes information presented by Dévora Kestel, Pan American Health Organization.

to change current practice. She remarked that, on the implementation side, she would like to see more linkage of evidence-based practices and practice-based evidence, as well as increased dissemination of those practices that have "worked enough."

She questioned whether deinstitutionalization had worked, as the idea of "putting people away" has not changed in the United States or elsewhere. People with mental illness are not receiving the community-based care they need, but instead still end up in institutions, whether psychiatric hospitals or prisons or others. She argued that this is a priority policy direction that needs greater uptake in all mental health disciplines. A comprehensive network of community-based mental health services, she opined, is the best way to prevent violence.

Influence of Violence on Mental Health[6]

James Mercy emphasized the importance of addressing the intersection of suicide and interpersonal violence, noting that one is not more important than the other, because several factors related to each overlap. He also pointed out that while suicide might result in greater mortality, the morbidity related to interpersonal violence should not be overlooked. Evidence is emerging that indicates the long-term effects of interpersonal violence, including chronic disease. It also has a strong impact on mental health: Exposure to violence in childhood is responsible for 30 percent of adult psychopathology (Kessler et al., 2010). Thus, he noted, it is important to look not only at the influence of mental health on violence but also at the influence of violence on mental health.

Mercy remarked that there are effective treatments to mitigate the effects of exposure to violence, but it is an area that needs more research into implementation and dissemination, particularly for scaling up in low- and middle-income countries. He also raised the question of whether these treatments could be considered primary prevention, since they might in the long run reduce interpersonal and self-directed violence.

Further research is needed, he concluded, in gathering better data linking mental health and the means of perpetrating violence and in what works in preventing violence related to mental illness, such as physician counseling or background checks.

---

[6] This section summarizes information presented by James Mercy, Centers for Disease Control and Prevention.

Brain, Behavior, and Targeted Interventions[7]

James Blair remarked that while another speaker had mentioned that population-based interventions achieve greater "bang for the buck," he believed there was an important role for individual-based interventions, as well. He cited an example of a school-based anti-bullying program in the United Kingdom that saw a reduction in rates of bullying, except in one group. The individuals in this group, he noted, are better suited for specific interventions to change underlying behavior; although screening tools are imperfect, they are somewhat useful for identifying these individuals.

Importantly, do current interventions actually work for these individuals? he queried. While some individuals do see a reduction in aggression with certain interventions, such as cognitive behavioral therapy (CBT), the neurobiological mechanisms are not clear. Blair commented that research to illuminate this mechanism more clearly, coupled with the overt behavioral change, would be important support in calling for additional resource allocation for these interventions. At the same time, there are individuals who do not respond as well to these interventions, so developing new interventions for them is an important priority.

Discussion

To close the workshop, participants shared their perspectives on the discussions over the 2 days and presented their thoughts on research, program implementation, and policy. Important questions were raised on:

- How to create constructive and ongoing collaboration, particularly among those with opposing political aims, that works toward a shared goal.
- How to mainstream some of the nontraditional approaches raised, such as therapeutic jurisprudence.
- How to end programs that do not work, expand those that do, and allocate resources for them.
- How to operationalize cross-cultural situational analysis, such as the role of science in policy, attitudes of policymakers, and incentivization of native providers, in developing countries.
- How to better adapt program evaluation designs that are truly fit for the purpose.
- How to create public buy-in to invest in dissemination of successful programs and program evaluation.

---

[7] This section summarizes information presented by James Blair, National Institute of Mental Health.

- How to harmonize data and data systems so that researchers who work from different angles can be more aware of evidence-based practices and instruments and access common data elements.

Participants shared additional lessons or approaches learned from their own experiences:

- Individuals at the highest risk of violence are also at the highest risk of re-offending. One participant remarked that the best intervention for this group might be to reach them at a young age; in particular, addressing the earliest stages of behavior through a better understanding of the precursors of both mental health and violence.
- Similarly, another participant noted that trauma early in life leads to sequela through the life span. Preventing that trauma could lead to a different developmental arc for those individuals.
- At the same time, treatments for posttraumatic stress disorder (PTSD) and other illnesses, such as attention deficit hyperactivity disorder (ADHD), do have measurable effects in the brain, so even those in the highest-risk groups for violence can be treated, even later in life. In particular, if treatment prevents reoccurrence of violence, it could be considered a form of prevention.
- A few participants discussed the potential for addressing the fear response and reactivity. There are several treatments, such as CBT, that reduce threat sensitivity and responsiveness in people with PTSD. These have implications for similar interventions in people with high levels of aggression.

REFERENCES

Kessler, R. C., K. A. McLaughlin, J. G. Green, M. J. Gruber, N. A. Sampson, A. M. Zaslavsky, S. Aguilar-Gaxiola, A. O. Alhamzawi, J. Alonso, M. Angermeyer, C. Benjet, E. Bromet, S. Chatterji, G. de Girolamo, K. Demyttenaere, J. Fayyad, S. Florescu, G. Gal, O. Gureje, J. M. Haro, C. Hu, E. B. Üstün, S. Vassilev, M. C. Viana, and D. R. Williams. 2010. Childhood adversities and adult psychopathology in the WHO World Mental Health Surveys. *British Journal of Psychiatry* 197(5):378–385.

NRC and IOM (National Research Council and Institute of Medicine). 2009. *Preventing mental, emotional, and behavioral disorders among young people: Progress and possibilities.* Washington, DC: The National Academies Press.

Appendix A

Workshop-Related Discussion Papers

CONTENTS

A.1 Neurocognitive Mechanisms Implicated in Increasing the Risk for Violence, *R. James R. Blair*   77

A.2 Violence and Mental Health: Opportunities for Prevention and Early Intervention, A Workshop of the National Academies of Sciences, Engineering, and Medicine's Forum on Global Violence Prevention, February 26, 2014, *Daniel Fisher*   84

A.3 Interface with the Justice Community: The Police, *Sheldon Greenberg*   90

A.4 Mental Health in Latin America and the Caribbean, *Dévora Kestel*   98

A.5 Heavy Episodic Alcohol Use and Intimate Partner Violence: A Cross-Cultural Public Health Issue, *Cory A. Crane and Kenneth E. Leonard*   106

A.6 Peer Bullying and Mental Health, *Dieter Wolke*   119

FIGURES AND TABLES

Figures

A-1 Mental health expenditures, 101
A-2 The impact of being bullied on functioning in adulthood, 121
A-3 Adjusted mean young adult CRP levels (mg/L) based on childhood/adolescent bullying status, 123

Tables

A-1 Mental Health Professionals in LAC, 102
A-2 Number of Users Attending Mental Health Facilities, 103

A.1

NEUROCOGNITIVE MECHANISMS IMPLICATED IN INCREASING THE RISK FOR VIOLENCE

R. James R. Blair[1]
[1] National Institute of Mental Health, Bethesda, MD

Correspondence to:
R. James R. Blair, PhD
9000 Rockville Pike
Bldg. 15k, Room 205, MSC 2670
Bethesda, MD 20892
jamesblair@mail.nih.gov

This work was supported by the Intramural Research Program of the National Institute of Mental Health, National Institutes of Health, under grant number 1-ZIA-MH002860 to James Blair.

The authors report no conflicts of interest.

Introduction:
Distinguishing Forms of Violence

The goal of this brief review is to consider neurocognitive mechanisms that, when dysfunctional, have been suggested to increase the risk for violence. However, before this can be considered it is worth noting that, from a neuroscience perspective, there appears to be more than one form of violence (Blair, 2001). Specifically, a distinction should be drawn between reactive (affective/defensive/impulsive) and instrumental (proactive/planned) aggression (Crick and Dodge, 1996).

Reactive aggression is unplanned and can be characterized as impulsive. It is explosive, involves the active confrontation of the victim and is typically accompanied by negative affect (anger, sadness, frustration, and irritation). One notable feature distinguishing reactive aggression in humans from that studied in animals is that in humans, it is often associated with frustration (Berkowitz, 1993). Frustration occurs when an individual continues to do an action in the expectation of a reward but does not actually receive that reward (Berkowitz, 1993).

Instrumental aggression in contrast is planned. It involves the selection of a behavior (a covert or overt aggressive response) in anticipation of a positive outcome (e.g., acquisition of territory or goods, improvement of social status, or gratification of a perceived need). Typically, there is an absence of accompanying intense emotion.

Different psychiatric conditions are associated with risks for different forms of aggression. Thus, patients with mood and anxiety conditions (e.g., posttraumatic stress disorder [PTSD]), as well as patients with intermittent explosive disorder (IED) and borderline personality disorder (BPD), are at increased risk for reactive aggression. In contrast, individuals with the personality disorder psychopathy, who show reduced guilt and empathy, show an increased risk for instrumental aggression coupled with an increased risk for reactive aggression (Frick et al., 2005). Importantly, a common pathophysiology likely underpins the increased risk for reactive aggression in PTSD, IED, and BPD (even if there are other aspects of pathophysiology that are idiosyncratic to the individual disorders). In contrast, a rather different pathophysiology likely underpins the increased risk for instrumental aggression in individuals with psychopathic traits.

A System Mediating Reactive Aggression: Acute Threat Response

The acute threat response involves freezing to a distal threat, fleeing if the threat approaches, and fighting if the threat is very proximal (Blanchard et al., 1977). As such, reactive aggression can be considered the ultimate response to extreme threat. Considerable work with animals has determined that the acute threat response is mediated by a neural circuit that runs from the medial amygdala downward, largely via the stria terminalis to the medial hypothalamus, and then the dorsal half of the periaqueductal gray (Panksepp, 1998; Gregg and Siegel, 2001). This circuitry is assumed to mediate reactive aggression in humans as well (Blair, 2001). In a healthy individual, a very high level of threat might initiate reactive aggression. However, it is suggested that certain clinical conditions lead to lower levels of threat having the same consequence. This is because prior priming of the circuitry, as a consequence of the clinical condition, means that a less intense threat is necessary to initiate reactive aggression (Blair, 2001).

Several psychiatric conditions show a significantly increased risk for reactive aggression. These include PTSD, IED, and BPD (Coccaro et al., 2007; New et al., 2009). In line with the suggestions above of a lowered threshold, patients with these clinical conditions all show heightened responsiveness of regions implicated in reactive aggression, particularly the amygdala, to emotional provocation (Coccaro et al., 2007; Lee et al., 2008; New et al., 2009). In addition, patients with BPD have also been found to show an increased amygdala response to interpersonal provocation (New et al., 2009).

Several psychosocial stressors, such as exposure to trauma and neglect, are known to selectively increase the risk for reactive aggression in humans (Crick and Dodge, 1996). Notably, these stressors have also been shown to increase the amygdala response to threat (McCrory et al., 2011; Tottenham et al., 2011). In short, it can be argued that these stressors increase the risk for reactive aggression because they increase the responsiveness of systems mediating the acute threat response. Because of this, the individual is more likely to display reactive aggression in response to future provocation.

Neurocognitive Mechanism That, When Dysfunctional, Increases the Risk for Instrumental Aggression: Empathic Responsiveness

An association between reduced empathic responsiveness to the distress of others and an increased risk for aggression has long been made (Miller and Eisenberg, 1988). Work has shown that empathic responses to the distress of others diminish aggressive responding (Perry and Perry, 1974). Moreover, empathic responding is critical for socialization. Caregivers most typically respond to transgressions that harm others by focusing on the distress of the victim (Nucci and Nucci, 1982). When this socialization is successful, the individual is less likely to choose actions that will harm others because of the aversive feelings he or she experiences in relation to the anticipated victim's distress.

Different definitions of empathy have been provided. But the functional processes, with respect to modulating the risk for aggression, concern the impact of distress cues (fearful, sad, and pained facial and vocal expressions) on (1) current behavior by interrupting it; and (2) future behavior by guiding, through social learning, the individual away from behavioral choices associated with harm to others. The amygdala is considered to be critical for both these processes. Considerable data show that the amygdala is responsive to fearful expressions (Adolphs, 2010) and, to a lesser extent, sad and pained expressions. Activation of the amygdala initiates freezing—interrupting current behavior. In addition, the amygdala is important for social learning. The amygdala enables the association of stimuli with the aversive reinforcement engendered by the fear of others (Jeon and Shin, 2011). This social learning means that the healthy individual comes to value actions that harm other individuals as aversive (Blair, 2013).

Deficient empathy is associated with conduct disorder (CD), particularly that associated with psychopathic traits, including reduced guilt (Blair, 2013). Such patients show reduced physiological responsiveness to expressions of distress in peers (Blair, 1999; de Wied et al., 2012). In addition, they show reduced amygdala responses to fearful and sad expressions, as well as the pain of others (Marsh et al., 2008; Viding et al., 2012; White et al., 2012). The presence of psychopathic traits, particularly reduced guilt and empathy, are associated with an increased risk for instrumental aggression (Cornell et al., 1996). The suggestion is that the individual with psychopathic traits is less likely to stop aggressing in response to the victim's distress because there is less amygdala activity and consequent freezing. In addition, such an individual is less guided away from actions that harm others because he or she has less learned the aversive value of actions that harm others. In line with this, individuals with psychopathic traits have been found to show greater indifference to transgressions that harm others (Aharoni, Antonenko, and Kiehl, 2011; Blair, 1995) and reduced amygdala responses to such transgressions (Glenn, Raine, and Schug, 2008). Such indifference means that the individual is more likely to commit an action that will harm others to achieve his or her goals.

Neurocognitive Mechanism That, When Dysfunctional, Increases the Risk for Reactive and Instrumental Aggression: Reward–Punishment-Based Decision Making

Problems in reward–punishment-based decision making are likely to increase the risk for reactive and instrumental aggression in several ways. First, individuals who fail to learn how to obtain rewards and avoid punishments through their decisions face high risk for impulsivity and frustration. Both impulsivity and frustration, in turn, predict risk for reactive aggression (Berkowitz, 1974). Second, it is suggested that systems involved in decision making are also involved in the regulation of the acute threat response. Specifically, ventromedial frontal cortex is involved in the selection of appropriate action as a function of the value outcomes associated with different behavioral choices (a critical component of reward–punishment-based decision making). An angry reactive response to provocation may not be selected if the negative value of the detrimental consequences of this action is appropriately represented (e.g., costs of imprisonment). Third, and relatedly, instrumental aggressive responses will be less likely to be selected if the negative values of their detrimental consequences are represented (e.g., victim's distress, and costs of imprisonment).

Systems neuroscience research links specific forms of decision making, involving reinforcement-based learning, to a circuit that connects the striatum, amygdala, and ventromedial frontal cortex as well as other structures (O'Doherty, 2012). Patients with conduct disorder exhibit a form of impaired decision making associated with dysfunction in this neural circuit. For example, they are more likely to respond to stimuli that engender punishment or continue to respond to stimuli that, while once rewarding, now engender punishment (Crowley et al., 2010; Finger et al., 2008; White et al.,

2013). Notably, such forms of impaired decision making occur in conduct disorder either with or without high levels of callous and unemotional traits (White et al., 2013), as well as in patients with ADHD without conduct disorder (Plichta et al., 2009; Scheres, Milham, Knutson, and Castellanos, 2007; Strohle et al., 2008). Moreover, they may occur in unaffected but at-risk children, born to parents with their own histories of conduct problems or drug addiction (Yau et al., 2012). Thus, impaired decision making arising from fronto-striatal dysfunction may represent a shared substrate for frequently comorbid disorders, such as conduct disorder, ADHD, and substance use disorders.

Conclusions

In conclusion, this review outlines three neurocognitive systems that, when dysfunctional, increase the risk for aggression. These are (1) the acute threat response implicating the amygdala, hypothalamus, and periaqueductal gray; (2) empathic responding (instrumental) implicating the amygdala and, in the context of decision making influenced by empathy for potential victims, ventromedial frontal cortex; and (3) reward–punishment-based decision making implicating striatum and ventromedial frontal cortex. Importantly, identifying these systems provides treatment targets. Interventions can be designed to address the functioning of these systems and their efficacy, indexed by their impact on the systems themselves, as well as downstream consequences of reduced aggression.

References

Adolphs, R. (2010). What does the amygdala contribute to social cognition? *Ann N Y Acad Sci, 1191*, 42-61. doi: 10.1111/j.1749-6632.2010.05445.x.

Aharoni, E., Antonenko, O., and Kiehl, K. A. (2011). Disparities in the moral intuitions of criminal offenders: The role of psychopathy. *J Res Pers, 45*(3), 322-327. doi: 10.1016/j.jrp.2011.02.005.

Berkowitz, L. (1993). *Aggression: Its causes, consequences, and control*. Philadelphia, PA: Temple University Press.

Berkowitz, L. (1974). Some determinants of impulsive aggression: Role of mediated associations with reinforcements for aggression. *Psychological Review, 81*, 165-176.

Blair, R. J. R. (1995). A cognitive developmental approach to morality: Investigating the psychopath. *Cognition, 57*, 1-29.

Blair, R. J. R. (2001). Neurocognitive models of aggression, the antisocial personality disorders, and psychopathy. *Journal of Neurology, Neurosurgery, and Psychiatry, 71*(6), 727-731.

Blair, R. J. (2013). The neurobiology of psychopathic traits in youths. *Nat Rev Neurosci, 14*(11), 786-799. doi: 10.1038/nrn3577.

Blair, R. J. R. (1999). Responsiveness to distress cues in the child with psychopathic tendencies. *Personality and Individual Differences, 27*, 135-145.

Blanchard, R. J., Blanchard, D. C., and Takahashi, L. K. (1977). Attack and defensive behaviour in the albino rat. *Animal Behavior, 25*, 197-224.

Blanchard, R. J., Takahashi, L. K., and Blanchard, D. C. (1977). The development of intruder attack in colonies of laboratory rats. *Animal Learning and Behavior, 5*(4), 365-369.

Coccaro, E. F., McCloskey, M. S., Fitzgerald, D. A., and Phan, K. L. (2007). Amygdala and orbitofrontal reactivity to social threat in individuals with impulsive aggression. *Biological Psychiatry, 62*(2), 168-178.

Cornell, D. G., Warren, J., Hawk, G., Stafford, E., Oram, G., and Pine, D. (1996). Psychopathy in instrumental and reactive violent offenders. *Journal of Consulting and Clinical Psychology, 64*, 783-790.

Crick, N. R., and Dodge, K. A. (1996). Social information-processing mechanisms in reactive and proactive aggression. *Child Development, 67*(3), 993-1002.

Crowley, T. J., Dalwani, M. S., Mikulich-Gilbertson, S. K., Du, Y. P., Lejuez, C. W., Raymond, K. M., and Banich, M. T. (2010). Risky decisions and their consequences: Neural processing by boys with Antisocial Substance Disorder. *PLoS ONE, 5*(9), e12835. doi: 10.1371/journal.pone.0012835.

de Wied, M., van Boxtel, A., Matthys, W., and Meeus, W. (2012). Verbal, facial and autonomic responses to empathy-eliciting film clips by disruptive male adolescents with high versus low callous-unemotional traits. *J Abnorm Child Psychol, 40*(2), 211-223. doi: 10.1007/s10802-011-9557-8.

Finger, E. C., Marsh, A. A., Mitchell, D. G. V., Reid, M. E., Sims, C., Budhani, S., . . . Blair, R. J. R. (2008). Abnormal ventromedial prefrontal cortex function in children with psychopathic traits during reversal learning. *Archives of General Psychiatry, 65*(5), 586-594.

Frick, P. J., Stickle, T. R., Dandreaux, D. M., Farrell, J. M., and Kimonis, E. R. (2005). Callous-unemotional traits in predicting the severity and stability of conduct problems and delinquency. *Journal of Abnormal Psychology, 33*(4), 471-487.

Glenn, A. L., Raine, A., and Schug, R. A. (2008). The neural correlates of moral decision-making in psychopathy. *Molecular Psychiatry, 14*, 5-6.

Gregg, T. R., and Siegel, A. (2001). Brain structures and neurotransmitters regulating aggression in cats: Implications for human aggression. *Prog Neuropsychopharmacol Biological Psychiatry, 25*(1), 91-140.

Jeon, D., and Shin, H. S. (2011). A mouse model for observational fear learning and the empathetic response. *Curr Protoc Neurosci, Chapter 8*, Unit 8 27. doi: 10.1002/0471142301.ns0827s57.

Lee, T. M. C., Chan, S. C., and Raine, A. (2008). Strong limbic and weak frontal activation to aggressive stimuli in spouse abusers. *Molecular Psychiatry, 13*(7), 655-656.

Marsh, A. A., Finger, E. C., Mitchell, D. G. V., Reid, M. E., Sims, C., Kosson, D. S., . . . Blair, R. J. R. (2008). Reduced amygdala response to fearful expressions in children and adolescents with callous-unemotional traits and disruptive behavior disorders. *American Journal of Psychiatry, 165*(6), 712-720.

McCrory, E. J., De Brito, S. A., Sebastian, C. L., Mechelli, A., Bird, G., Kelly, P. A., and Viding, E. (2011). Heightened neural reactivity to threat in child victims of family violence. *Curr Biol, 21*(23), R947-948. doi: 10.1016/j.cub.2011.10.015.

Miller, P. A., and Eisenberg, N. (1988). The relation of empathy to aggressive and externalizing/antisocial behavior. *Psychological Bulletin, 103*, 324-344.

New, A. S., Hazlett, E. A., Newmark, R. E., Zhang, J., Triebwasser, J., Meyerson, D., Lazarus, S., Trisdorfer, R., Goldstein, K. E., Goodman, M., Koenigsberg, H. W., Flory, J. D., Siever, L. J., and Buchsbaum, M. S. (2009). Laboratory induced aggression: A positron emission tomography study of aggressive individuals with borderline personality disorder. *Biological Psychiatry, 66*(12), 1107-1114.

Nucci, L. P., and Nucci, M. (1982). Children's social interactions in the context of moral and conventional transgressions. *Child Development, 53,* 403-412.
O'Doherty, J. P. (2012). Beyond simple reinforcement learning: The computational neurobiology of reward learning and valuation. *Eur J Neurosci, 15*(7), 987-990. doi: 10.1111/j.1460-9568.2012.08074.x.
Panksepp, J. (1998). *Affective neuroscience: The foundations of human and animal emotions.* New York: Oxford University Press.
Perry, D. G., and Perry, L. C. (1974). Denial of suffering in the victim as a stimulus to violence in aggressive boys. *Child Development, 45,* 55-62.
Plichta, M. M., Vasic, N., Wolf, R. C., Lesch, K. P., Brummer, D., Jacob, C., . . . Gron, G. (2009). Neural hyporesponsiveness and hyperresponsiveness during immediate and delayed reward processing in adult attention-deficit/hyperactivity disorder. *Biol Psychiatry, 65*(1), 7-14. doi: 10.1016/j.biopsych.2008.07.008.
Scheres, A., Milham, M. P., Knutson, B., and Castellanos, F. X. (2007). Ventral striatal hyporesponsiveness during reward anticipation in attention-deficit/hyperactivity disorder. *Biol Psychiatry, 61*(5), 720-724. doi: 10.1016/j.biopsych.2006.04.042.
Strohle, A., Stoy, M., Wrase, J., Schwarzer, S., Schlagenhauf, F., Huss, M., . . . Heinz, A. (2008). Reward anticipation and outcomes in adult males with attention-deficit/hyperactivity disorder. *Neuroimage, 39*(3), 966-972. doi: 10.1016/j.neuroimage.2007.09.044.
Tottenham, N., Hare, T. A., Millner, A., Gilhooly, T., Zevin, J. D., and Casey, B. J. (2011). Elevated amygdala response to faces following early deprivation. *Dev Sci, 14*(2), 190-204. doi: 10.1111/j.1467-7687.2010.00971.x.
Viding, E., Sebastian, C. L., Dadds, M. R., Lockwood, P. L., Cecil, C. A., De Brito, S. A., and McCrory, E. J. (2012). Amygdala response to preattentive masked fear in children with conduct problems: The role of callous-unemotional traits. *Am J Psychiatry, 169*(10), 1109-1116. doi: 10.1176/appi.ajp.2012.12020191.
White, S. F., Marsh, A. A., Fowler, K. A., Schechter, J. C., Adalio, C., Pope, K., . . . Blair, R. J. R. (2012). Reduced amygdala responding in youth with disruptive behavior disorder and psychopathic traits reflects a reduced emotional response not increased top-down attention to non-emotional features. *American Journal of Psychiatry, 169*(7), 750-758.
White, S. F., Pope, K., Sinclair, S., Fowler, K. A., Brislin, S. J., Williams, W. C., . . . Blair, R. J. R. (2013). Disrupted expected value and prediction error signaling in youth with disruptive behavior disorders during a passive avoidance task. *American Journal of Psychiatry.*
Yau, W. Y., Zubieta, J. K., Weiland, B. J., Samudra, P. G., Zucker, R. A., and Heitzeg, M. M. (2012). Nucleus accumbens response to incentive stimuli anticipation in children of alcoholics: Relationships with precursive behavioral risk and lifetime alcohol use. *J Neurosci, 32*(7), 2544-2551. doi: 10.1523/jneurosci.1390-11.2012.

A.2

VIOLENCE AND MENTAL HEALTH: OPPORTUNITIES FOR PREVENTION AND EARLY INTERVENTION, A WORKSHOP OF THE NATIONAL ACADEMIES OF SCIENCES, ENGINEERING, AND MEDICINE'S FORUM ON GLOBAL VIOLENCE PREVENTION, FEBRUARY 26, 2014

Daniel Fisher

Presentation by Daniel Fisher, M.D.,
Executive Director, National Empowerment Center,
25 Bigelow St., Cambridge, MA 02139

The very title of this conference saddens me, and makes me angry. Clearly the gun lobby has been effective in changing the narrative from controlling guns to controlling those of us who have been labeled mentally ill. This narrative is based on false information equating persons with mental health disorders with increased violence.

Introduction

In my 20s I was diagnosed with schizophrenia and was involuntarily hospitalized on three occasions. Ironically, I was studying the possible biochemical bases of mental illnesses at the National Institute of Mental Health (NIMH) at the time. (That was in the late '60s. In May of last year, 45 years later, Dr. Thomas Insel of NIMH stated that NIMH will not use the *Diagnostic and Statistical Manual of Mental Disorders, Fifth Edition* [DSM-5] because its diagnostic categories are not based on biological markers.) I was researching the factors controlling the biosynthesis of dopamine and serotonin. I so reduced human experiences to chemistry that I became convinced that we all were merely chemical machines, and that we lacked meaning or agency. I lost the meaning of human relationships and emotional expression. Being unable to understand communication left me out of touch. I believe this empty view of life and the loneliness it produced left me in despair and caused me to depart from everyday reality. I indeed did fit the DSM definition of schizophrenia. I recovered from schizophrenia by finding meaning through emotionally connecting with others and myself. I concluded that we have a self that supersedes all we can write in a formula. This understanding brought me back to everyday life with people. I decided I could learn more about this human dimension by becoming a psychiatrist, and have practiced in clinical settings for the last 35 years. I also founded and run the National Empowerment Center, a Substance Abuse and Mental Health Services Administration (SAMHSA)-funded, technical assistance center dedicated to bringing hope and recovery to the mental health system and society.

Recovery depends on people with mental illness finding meaningful relationships and working in the community. The misinformation perpetuated by our media is interfering with recovery. This incorrect coupling of mental health issues with violence increases prejudice and discrimination among all members of society. (Advocates are rejecting the use of the term "stigma" because the term itself has produced increased prejudice.)

I will summarize the evidence that people diagnosed with mental health conditions are no more violent than matched community members without such a label. Although there is a lack of association of violence and mental health conditions, the increased attention on mental health can be an opportunity to improve that system. Therefore, I will point out problems in our mental health system and society that are barriers to recovery. Finally, I will recommend ways that our mental health system needs to continue its transformation from a maintenance-based to a recovery-based system.

The Evidence Does Not Link Persons with Mental Health Disorders to Violence

A recently published report by the Consortium for Risk-Based Firearm Policy (2013) concluded: "Research evidence shows that the large majority of people with mental illness do not engage in violence against others and most violence is caused by factors other than mental illness." **The report also found that "research evidence suggests that . . . mental illness alone rarely causes violence."** These conclusions were based on three studies (Elbogen and Johnson, 2009; Swanson et al., 2013; Van Dorn et al., 2012).

This evidence fits closely with the findings of the MacArthur Violence Risk Assessment Study, considered one of the most definitive published studies of mental health issues and violence. Dr. Heather Stuart (summarized the MacArthur Study as follows: The MacArthur Violence Risk Assessment Study (Applebaum et al., 2000; Monahan et al., 2001; Steadman et al., 1998, 2000) "has made a concerted effort to address . . . [methodological] problems, so it stands out as the most sophisticated attempt to date to disentangle these complex interrelationships" (Stuart, 2003).

> Because they collected extensive follow-up data on a large cohort of subject (N = 1,136), the temporal sequencing of important events is clear. Because they used multiple measures of violence, including patient self-report, they have minimized the information bias characterizing past work. The innovative use of same-neighbor comparison subjects eliminates confound-

ing from broad environmental influences such as socio-demographic or economic factors that may have exaggerated differences in past research.

In this study, the prevalence of violence among those with a major mental disorder who did not abuse substances was indistinguishable from their non-substance abusing neighborhood controls. Delusions were not associated with violence, even 'threat control override' delusions that cause an individual to think that someone is out to harm them or that someone can control their thoughts. (Stuart, 2003)

Fazel and colleagues (Fazel et al., 2009a), carried out a meta-analysis of 20 studies that examined a possible relationship of violence to mental health conditions. They concluded that "psychosis comorbid with substance abuse confers no additional risk over and above the risk associated with substance abuse." This finding was consistent with their own finding that schizophrenia, in the absence of substance abuse, did not increase the risk of violence when compared to the general population (Fazel et al., 2009b).

Therefore, every significant research study carried out starting with the MacArthur Study in the late 1990s has concluded that:

1. Persons with mental illness are no more likely than the matched controls in the community [to perform violent acts].
2. Persons with a substance abuse disorder carry a substantial risk of increased violence.

Therefore, "**Strategies that aim to reduce gun violence by focusing . . . on restricting access to guns by those diagnosed with a mental illness are unlikely to reduce the overall rate of gun violence in the United States**" (Consortium for Risk-Based Firearm Policy, 2013).

The National Instant Background Check System, NICS, should be focused on dangerousness and a history of violence rather than a mental health diagnosis per se (Consortium for Risk-Based Firearm Policy, 2013). After all, those of us diagnosed with a mental health disorder account for only 4 percent of the gun-related homicides (Swanson et al., 2013).

Our Mental Health System Is Not a Welcoming Place

It is dehumanizing, and hope-robbing approaches are major reasons why it is broken. It could practice hospitality, like hotels, through the practice of dialogue. Instead it practices varying degrees of coercion, persuasion, and suggestion. These all are forms of trauma. To be trauma-informed, we need to adhere to principles of dialogue emphasizing connecting, especially at the emotional level, mutual respect for the full humanity of the person in distress and listening to his or her voice, believing in them, and giving them hope and humility. Peers can greatly enhance these qualities when their roles as recovery coaches are valued and understood.

Our Deeper Malaise

Rather than focus on our mental health system alone, I want to point out that dehumanizing labels and coercion are a reflection of a deeper woe, that is, the breakdown of cohesion in our communities. The fear in our society of people who are different or odd is the basis for such reactions. We desperately need to rebuild positive connections to each other in our communities. Cross-cultural studies have shown that contact with people of differing race and culture, as well as mental health issues, is a critical factor in becoming more comfortable with them. Contact also decreases prejudice, stigma, and discrimination.

Recommendations

1. Broaden the community dialogue on mental health, and ensure that persons with lived experience of mental health conditions are included in the planning and participation of these dialogues.
2. NIMH and SAMHSA should promote the training and evaluation of Open Dialogue (Seikkula, 2006) in the United States, to reach people where they live, and while they are still connected to their natural supports. This approach, developed in Finland, is the most successful approach in the world for helping young people who have experienced their first psychotic experience to recover a full life in the community.
3. Hiring peers in valued roles as crisis workers and in peer-run respites; peers are capable of reaching persons whom non-peers cannot reach. This is true because when you have experienced delusions and voices, you know how to reach and connect with other persons going through a similar experience. Peer-run respites are a good example of the application of this capacity of peers in diverting persons from hospitalization (see the section on crisis respites at www.power2u.org).
4. Training first responders, peers, and families in Emotional CPR. This is a preventative public health program, enabling anyone to help another person through an emotional crisis. eCPR, therefore, represents the type of primary prevention that would reach a much greater proportion of persons than present programs that focus on persons labeled with mental health disorders (see www.emotional-cpr.org).

5. Speakers sharing recovery stories in person with media officials, police, parents, and other important community groups. Research has shown that the most effective way to reduce prejudice and discrimination is through people sharing their stories (Corrigan, 2005).
6. Educating the media to not continue the misinformation of links between mental health issues and violence (the "See Me" campaign in Scotland is a good example of this media education).
7. Continue the transformation from a medical narrative to a recovery narrative that was started in the Surgeon General's Mental Health Report (1999) and the New Freedom Commission (Fisher, 2008; New Freedom Commission on Mental Health, 2003).

Comments on Other Talks Given at the National Academies of Sciences, Engineering, and Medicine's Workshop on Violence and Mental Health

Dr. Paul Appelbaum pointed out that Wayne LaPierre, vice president of the National Rifle Association (NRA), quickly shifted the blame for the Sandy Hook shootings in December 2012 from guns to persons labeled with mental illness. He said that the problem of gun violence is not guns but people with mental illness, whom he described as "deranged mongrels." The NRA called for ensuring that persons labeled with mental illness be placed on the National Instant Criminal Background Check System (NICS). This represented a change in policy of the NRA, which as recently as 2007, had loosened the NICS: "The price for bringing the NRA on board [for the NICS bill of 2007] was to take the 'mentally ill' tag away from anyone 'rehabilitated through any procedure available under law' and to enact a 'Relief from Disabilities' reform. The latter reform allowed people classified as mentally ill, and unable to buy guns, to get their rights back with more ease" (Weigel, 2013).

References

Appelbaum, P.S., Robbins, P.C., Monahan, J. 2000.Violence and delusions: Data from the MacArthur Violence Risk Assessment Study. *Am. J. Psychiatry* 157:566-572.

Consortium for Risk-Based Firearm Policy. 2013. *Guns, public health and mental illness: An evidence-based approach for state policy.* John Hopkins University: Baltimore, MD.

Corrigan, P. 2005. *On the stigma of mental illness: Implications for research and social change, fifth edition.* American Psychological Association: Washington, DC.

Elbogen, E., and Johnson, S. 2009. Intricate link between violence and mental disorder results from national epidemiological survey on alcohol and related conditions. *Archives General Psychiatry* 66:152-161.

Fazel, S., Gulati, G., Linsell, L., Geddes, J.R., and Grann, M. 2009. Schizophrenia and violence: Systematic review and meta-analysis. *PLoS Med* 6(8): e1000120. doi:10.1371/journal.pmed.1000120.

Fazel, S., Landstrom, N., Hjern, A., Grann, M., and Lichtenstein, P. 2009. Schizophrenia, substance abuse, and violent crime. *JAMA* 301(19):2016-2023.

Fisher, D.B. 2008. *Promoting recovery. Learning about mental health practice.* Eds. T. Stickley and T. Basset. John Wiley and Sons: Chichester, U.K. pp. 119-139.

McGinty, E., et al. 2013. Gun policy and serious mental illness: Priorities for future research and policy. *Psychiatric Services*, epub ahead of print, doi:10.1176/appi. Ps.201300141.

Monahan, J., Steadman, H.J., Silver, E., et al. 2001. *Risk assessment: the MacArthur Study of Mental Disorder and Violence.* Oxford University Press: Oxford, U.K.

New Freedom Commission on Mental Health. 2003. *Achieving the promise: Transforming mental health care in America final report.* DHHS Pub. No. SMA-03-3832. U.S. Department of Health and Human Services: Rockville, MD.

Seikkula, J., and Trimble, D. 2005. Healing elements of therapeutic conversation: Dialogue as an embodiment of love. *Family Process* 44(4):461-475.

Seikkula, J., Aaltonen, K., Alakare, B., Haarakanga, K., Keranen, J., and Lehtinen, K. 2006. Five-year experience of first-episode nonaffective psychosis in open-dialogue approach: Treatment principles, follow-up outcomes, and two case studies. *Psychotherapy Research* 16(2):214-228.

Steadman, H.J., Silver, E., Monahan, J., Appelbaum, P.S., et al. 2000. A classification tree approach to the development of actuarial violence risk-assessment tools. *Law Humanity Behavior* 24:83-100.

Steadman, H.J., Mulvy, E.P., Monahan, J., et al. 1998. Violence by people discharged from acute psychiatric inpatient facilities and by others in the same neighborhoods. *Arch Gen Psychiatry* 55:393-404.

Stuart, H. 2003. Violence and mental illness: An overview. *World Psychiatric Assoc* 2:121-124.

Swanson, J. et al. 2013. "Preventing gun violence involving people with serious mental illness." In *Reducing gun violence in America: Informing policy with evidence and analysis.* Webster, D. and Vernick, J. eds. Johns Hopkins University Press: Baltimore, MD. pp. 33-51.

U.S. Department of Health and Human Services. 1999. Mental health: A report of the Surgeon General. U.S. Department of Health and Human Services, Substance Abuse and Mental Health Services Administration, Center for Mental Health Services, National Institutes of Health, National Institute of Mental Health: Rockville, MD.

Van Dorn, R., Volavka, J., and Johnson, N. 2012. Mental disorder and violence: Is there a relationship beyond substance abuse? *Social Psychiatry and Psychiatric Epidemiology* 47:487-503.

Weigel, D. 2013. CPAC Diary: Wayne LaPierre's "Mental Health" Chutzpah. *Slate* Magazine, March 15.

A.3

INTERFACE WITH THE JUSTICE COMMUNITY: THE POLICE

Sheldon Greenberg, Ph.D.
Johns Hopkins University

Despite the long-term call by criminal justice and mental health professionals, advocates, and political officials to work together more effectively in providing services to people with mental illness, progress in many jurisdictions (cities, counties, towns, states, tribal land) and nations has been slow. This paper presents and expands on a portion of the information presented during the workshop titled Mental Health and Violence: Opportunities for Prevention and Early Intervention. It offers information on the interface between the criminal justice and mental health communities, addresses some of the reasons for measured progress, and suggests ways in which the two professions might advance success. While this paper briefly addresses public safety, including corrections, it focuses primarily on interaction among the police, mental health providers, and people who have mental illness and their families, friends, and other advocates.

For decades, mental health professionals, advocacy organizations, family members, political leaders, and others have sought to have the criminal justice system or criminal justice community (generally perceived as consisting of the police, courts, and corrections) end the unnecessary "criminalization" of mental illness. This continues to be a priority.

Generally, an arrest is defined as the taking of a person into custody by a legal authority, usually in response to a criminal charge. The criminalization hypothesis is based on the assumption that police inappropriately use arrest to resolve encounters with people who have mental illness (Engel and Silver, 2001). Criminalization that can affect the future of a person with mental illness goes beyond traditional arrest and may include criminal citations (usually issued for minor offenses that do not require taking a person into custody) and inclusion of names in criminal incident reports.

Terms such as "criminal justice system" and "criminal justice community" suggest that there is a common foundation of standards, policies, practices, and other linkages across the profession. In fact, criminal justice in the United States and in many other nations is a highly fragmented, parochial, and compartmentalized and, at times, is a competitive collection of local, state, tribal, and federal agencies. There is no central organization, professional association, or other body with the authority to mandate policy, practice, or change. As of 2011, there were approximately 15,000 local police departments in the United States. The majority of these agencies have fewer than 25 personnel. Fewer than 70 agencies serve jurisdictions with large populations (500,000 or more) (Baltic, 2011). Fragmentation exists in other nations as well, although some nations have a single national police force (France, Italy, Japan, New Zealand, Nicaragua) or a small number of agencies (Sweden, United Kingdom), and other nations' law enforcement services are provided by their defense agency/military (Chilean Carabineros).

For a brief perspective on the larger justice system in the United States, there are 3,365 local jails, not including state, federal, military, or juvenile correctional institutions. Data on the number of courts—federal, state, local, military, and specialized—are weak, although it is estimated that there are more than 3,000 trial court judges serving the nation. The global criminal justice system is diverse, and the concept of justice (fair processes, just outcomes, respect for human rights and dignity, upholding law) is too varied and complex in some nations and ill-defined in others to describe adequately in this paper (Nagel, 2005).

Since the period of deinstitutionalization (intended to close large, often antiquated public mental health hospitals and ensure the transfer of patients to community-based mental health services) that began in the mid-1950s and increased continually through the 1980s, criminal justice agencies have altered policies, procedures, training, and relationships with mental health providers and advocates to overcome difficulties stemming from critical and routine interaction with people who have severe mental illness (Lurigio and Swartz, 2000). When deinstitutionalization began in 1955, there were approximately 560,000 severely mentally ill patients in the nation's public psychiatric hospitals. By 1994, this number was reduced by more than 485,000 patients to approximately 72,000 (Frontline, 2005). Several failed federal acts and the weak community response to supporting those who returned to the community placed new and immediate burdens on the police, courts, and corrections. Similar experiences occurred in other nations and continents, including Australia, New Zealand, and Western Europe (Fakhoury and Priebe, 2002). Two significant consequences of deinstitutionalization have been the "criminalization of mental illness" (Peternelj-Taylor, 2008) and victimization of people who have mental illness (Teplin et al., 2005).

In considering the interface with the criminal justice system by mental health providers, public health, social services, the faith community, and other organizations, it is essential to focus on the role of the frontline police officer as the "point of entry" and "point of diversion" toward or away from arrest, prosecution, and incarceration. Generally, a police officer's decision to connect with a mental health service provider or other support service, arrest (criminalize), pursue hospitalization or other placement, or handle the call informally is based primarily on the characteristics and constraints of each situation rather than the symptomatology or awareness of mental illness (Lamb et al., 2002; Teplin, 2000). Action and decisions by prosecutors and the courts will be determined, in great part, by the actions and reports of the responding police officers.

Police agencies have sought to improve response to calls for service and other incidents involving people with mental illness, especially those considered crisis or emergency situations. These new developments (training, advances in policy, scrutiny of arrests, crisis intervention teams), however, have been targeted almost exclusively at improved handling of individual incidents. Less attention has been devoted to developing or implementing comprehensive, multiagency, and preventive approaches (Cordner, 2006).

Generally, police become involved in situations and interact with people who have mental illness when problems surface (Cordner, 2006). One three-city study found that 92 percent of uniformed patrol officers had at least one interaction with a person experiencing a mental health crisis in the previous month. Police officers report that they are involved in an average of six calls per month specifically related to people with mental illness (Borum, 2000; Vermette et al., 2005). An estimated 7 percent of police contacts in jurisdictions with 100,000 or more involve people with mental illness (Deane et al., 1999). The above data are based on reported incidents. A significant percentage of a police officer's interaction, intervention, and problem-solving activity never makes its way into police reports and is never captured in the data. Such activity is not found in the reported data for several reasons: the situation requiring police intervention may have been resolved quickly or informally; the officer did not want the involved individuals to be named in a report; and/or the information may have been recorded according to the initial call (assault, domestic situation, suspicious activity, injured person), with no identifiers related to mental illness. In some cases, the officer simply may have chosen not to file a formal report.

Research shows consistently that police officers do not want to criminalize events involving people with mental illness unless significant violation of the law has occurred (assault, theft, arson, weapons violation) and cannot be ignored or handled less formally. Officers express frustration in handling calls involving people with mental illness because of the lack of needed information, the lack of immediately available resources, and the lack of coordination in effort between police and mental health professionals (Engel and Silver, 2001; Novak and Engel, 2005; Wells and Schafer, 2006).

There is minimal research on the face-to-face interaction among the first-responding patrol officer, the person who has mental illness, family members, and others. Little is known about what occurs in the first moments of a situation that drives the involved players toward pursuing informal de-escalation, or more formal interventions, such as criminalization, a call for response by mental health professionals, commitment/hospitalization, or other interventions or diversions from the criminal justice system (Tucker, Hasselt, and Russell, 2008).

Notable progress was made with the establishment of Crisis Intervention Teams (CITs) in the late 1980s, which brought together well-trained police officers and mental health professionals to respond immediately to calls for service involving people who have mental illness. Although recognized primarily for intervention in serious or critical situations, CITs responded to any call (crisis and non-critical) in which the caller or responding police officer identified the need for support. These teams primarily appeared in urban and metropolitan environments—Baltimore County, Charlotte-Mecklenburg, Los Angeles, Memphis, and Milwaukee—which had the demand and resources to support them. In some of these jurisdictions, police officers received 40 hours of instruction or more on intervention strategies and often participated in joint training with mental health workers.

Officers who received the training and were assigned to CITs reported improved ability to recognize and respond to calls involving people with mental illness, reduced stereotyping, greater empathy, improved ability to resolve the situation, better communication skills, and increased patience. They further reported that they were less likely to arrest and more prone to redirect the individual toward other forms of support (Hanafi et al., 2008). Importantly, research shows that officers trained to participate in CITs or who received comparable training regarding mental health intervention were less likely than their peers, in some situations, to use force or perceive escalating force as effective in dealing with a person who has mental illness (Compton et al., 2009).

Access to CITs in the United States began declining in recent years, along with other support services, due to local budget crises and federal cost containment strategies (Cunningham et al., 2006). Expansion of CITs is questionable for the foreseeable future.

Training for police personnel remains a void in improving criminal justice service to people who have mental illness. Data on the number of police officers trained are unreliable since some agencies train more than those needed to serve on CITs, and others, especially smaller agencies, rely on other organizations to train their employees. Some agencies do not keep comprehensive data on training provided to their employees. Some states and larger agencies have sought to provide mental health intervention training to a minimum of 20 percent of their officers (Compton et al., 2008). To date, there has been minimal research assessing the quality of CIT and other mental health training provided to police officers, its endurance over time, or the impact it has on outcomes for people who have mental illness and their families (Lord et al., 2011).

Officers assigned to CITs receive training that surpasses the norm for their peers. A survey of 33 state law enforcement certification agencies (Police Officer Standards and Training Commissions [POSTs]), which exist in almost every state in the United States, showed that the average training for police officers on "mental illness" was 9.1 hours. The majority of training courses ranged from 2 to 4 hours, with the shortest course being 50 minutes. These courses included content on awareness and process (policies and procedures for arrest, safety, and commitment to a hospital, shelter, or other care facility). Some of the courses described by the states incorporated mental illness with training on all "special populations," with no information on time allotted specifically to mental illness. Two states reported that they have no requirement for training on mental illness. Little research is available on training provided to specialized police agencies, such as school police, campus police and security personnel, transportation police, and tribal police. The inconsistency in and minimal amount of training provided to police on service to people who have mental illness is a global issue (Psarra et al., 2008).

Calls are made to the police by people with mental illness who have been victimized, as well as by spouses, other family members, neighbors, mental health professionals, and people who simply observe behavior or an incident but have no relationship to the person with mental illness. The importance of the initial point of contact—often a police or other government call taker/dispatcher—in obtaining critical information and relaying it to the responding police patrol officer cannot be overstated. Despite improved police call-taking protocols, information provided to the police call taker by the victim or observer (witness) is too often brief, panicked, incomplete, and inaccurate. They may only report the immediate need, threat, or danger and fail to mention that a person who has mental illness is involved. As such, the initial information a police officer receives may make no reference to mental illness or contain any details about risk, existing injury or illness, medication use, illicit substance abuse, presence of weapons, or precise location. Officers need, but often lack, information on the individual's medical or criminal history, cause of the crisis or hostility, prior suicide or self-injury attempts, and attending physicians, among other information (James, 1990). Information provided to a responding police officer may be described as and limited to the following:

- Man injured
- Woman acting out
- Doctor has trouble with patient
- Unknown trouble
- Suspicious circumstance
- Assault

- Threat of assault
- Threat of suicide
- Parent cannot control child
- Disorderly conduct
- Assist with a commitment

Officer safety and the safety of others are paramount when police officers receive a call for service or personally observe an unusual behavior. When information about mental illness is conveyed, no matter how detailed, police officers make assumptions about the potential for danger (Watson et al., 2004).

Lack of Information and Need for Research on Initial Points of Contact

Much of what occurs—including police officers' discretionary decision making to criminalize or divert from criminalization—is based on the observed behavior, early formulation of perceptions, and communication that occurs in the early moments of the situation. Yet, little is known about the nature and quality of the initial face-to-face interaction of police officers called into situations involving people who have mental illness. Conclusions and assumptions about the early one-on-one interaction that occur are drawn from police incident report narratives, interviews, anecdotal information, and, to a lesser degree, statistical reports, policies and procedures, and training curricula.

There is minimal research on the initial face-to-face interaction (point of contact) between police officers and people who have mental illness. There is little research on the initial interaction between responding police officers and spouses, family members, neighbors, and other involved parties. There is little research on how information conveyed early in a situation might influence, positively or negatively, the re-criminalization of a person with mental illness who had prior contact with the criminal justice system. Research is needed to answer key questions that can possibly lead to more positive courses of action for people with mental illness who are victimized, accused, or perceived as being dangerous to themselves or others:

- What is the level of understanding about the situation by the responding officer before he or she arrives?
- What facts were conveyed to the police department by the caller, and how was this information relayed to the responding officer?
- At what point in the situation does awareness of mental illness become known?
- What co-occurring factors (injury, illicit substance abuse) were apparent at the immediate point of contact?

- What was the real or perceived level of risk of harm (presence of weapons, threats), and how did it evolve?
- How emotional or tense was the situation upon the officer's arrival?
- What words or actions by the dispatcher, family members, witnesses, and people who have mental illness set the course for police action, particularly the criminalizing or decriminalizing of the situation?
- To what degree did the immediate situation allow for alternatives to criminalization?
- Was information shared about prior history, including incarceration or hospitalization, and what influence did this have on the initial thinking and action by the responding police officer(s)?
- Was the availability (readiness at the time of need) of mental health service providers known to the initial responding officer(s)?
- At what point did police officers connect with a mental health service provider, and what was the nature of their initial information sharing and action planning?

Other Needs to Improve Police Interaction

Other needs and recommendations to improve interaction between the police and people who have mental illness were discussed during a roundtable discussion with public safety practitioners held at The Johns Hopkins University (Division of Public Safety Leadership, 2013). The following reflects some of these needs and recommendations. Due to space limitation, the following recommendations are noted in brief:

- Improved methods for conveying research to frontline practitioners
- Research on point-of-contact communication and other characteristics of initial interaction that influence outcomes
- Orientation/training for mental health professionals on public safety and, particularly, the police (culture, fragmentation, training, policy, safety mandates, discretion, liability)
- Research on the curricula being used to teach the police, with attention to awareness, interaction, use of community-based resources, and law
- Model curricula for police, designed to accommodate the various time limitations imposed by police academy schedules
- Model curricula for police on how to manage concurrent issues (mental illness, mobility or communication disability, criminal behavior, homelessness, substance abuse, injury)
- Model curricula on interacting with people with mental illness who are victimized

- Research on successes, beyond crisis intervention teams, particularly those related to informal diffusion of situations and those in which criminalization did not occur
- Model training and awareness programs, supported by marketing strategies, to educate people who have mental illness and their support network (spouse, family, friends) on interacting with the police, particularly during initial contact
- Advancing call-taker protocols to obtain more and better information from callers to relay to responding police officers and, where joint response occurs, mental health workers or CITs

References

Baltic, S. E. (Ed.). (2011). *Crime in the United States 2011*. Bernan Press.

Borum, R. (2000). Improving high-risk encounters between people with mental illness and the police. *The Journal of the American Academy of Psychiatry and the Law, 28*(3), 332-337.

Compton, M. T., Bahora, M., Watson, A. C., and Oliva, J. R. (2008). A comprehensive review of extant research on Crisis Intervention Team (CIT) programs. *Journal of the American Academy of Psychiatry and the Law Online, 36*(1), 47-55.

Compton, M. T., Neubert, B. N. D., Broussard, B., McGriff, J. A., Morgan, R., and Oliva, J. R. (2009). Use of force preferences and perceived effectiveness of actions among Crisis Intervention Team (CIT) police officers and non-CIT officers in an escalating psychiatric crisis involving a subject with schizophrenia. *Schizophrenia Bulletin*, sbp146.

Cordner, G. (2006). People with mental illness. *Problem-oriented guides for police, Problem-Specific Guides Series* (40).

Cunningham, P., McKenzie, K., and Taylor, E. F. (2006). The struggle to provide community-based care to low-income people with serious mental illnesses. *Health Affairs, 25*(3), 694-705.

Deane, M. W., Steadman, H. J., Borum, R., Veysey, B. M., and Morrissey. J. P. (1999). Emerging partnerships between mental health and law enforcement. *Psychiatric Services, 50*(1), 99-101.

Division of Public Safety Leadership. (2013). *Roundtable on Police response to People with Mental Illness*. Johns Hopkins University, School of Education, Division of Public Safety Leadership, March 19, 2013, Columbia, Maryland.

Engel, R. S., and Silver, E. (2001). Policing mentally disordered suspects: A reexamination of the criminalization hypothesis. *Criminology, 39*(2), 225-252.

Fakhoury, W., and Priebe, S. (2002). The process of deinstitutionalization: An international overview. *Current Opinion in Psychiatry, 15*(2), 187-192.

Frontline. (2005). *Deinstitutionalization: A Psychiatric "Titanic."* Retrieved from http://www.pbs.org/wgbh/pages/frontline/shows/asylums/special/excerpt.html.

Hanafi, S., Bahora, M., Demir, B. N., and Compton, M. T. (2008). Incorporating crisis intervention team (CIT) knowledge and skills into the daily work of police officers: A focus group study. *Community Mental Health Journal, 44*(6), 427-432.

James, R. (1990). What do police officers really want from the mental health system? *Hospital and Community Psychiatry, 41*(6), 663.

Lamb, H. R., Weinberger, L. E., and DeCuir, W. J. (2002). The police and mental health. *Psychiatric Services, 53*(10), 1266-1271.

Lord, V. B., Bjerregaard, B., Blevins, K. R., and Whisman, H. (2011). Factors influencing the responses of crisis intervention team–certified law enforcement officers. *Police Quarterly, 14*(4), 388-406.

Lurigio, A. J., and Swartz, J. A. (2000). Changing the contours of the criminal justice system to meet the needs of persons with serious mental illness. *Criminal Justice, 3,* 45-108.

Nagel, T. (2005). The problem of global justice. *Philosophy and Public Affairs, 33*(2), 113-147.

Novak, K. J., and Engel, R. S. (2005). Disentangling the influence of suspects' demeanor and mental disorder on arrest. *Policing: An International Journal of Police Strategies and Management, 28*(3), 493-512.

Peternelj-Taylor, C. (2008). Criminalization of the mentally ill. *Journal of Forensic Nursing, 4*(4), 185-187.

Psarra, V., Sestrini, M., Santa, Z., Petsas, D., Gerontas, A., Garnetas, C., and Kontis, K. (2008). Greek police officers' attitudes towards the mentally ill. *International Journal of Law and Psychiatry, 31*(1), 77-85.

Teplin, L. A. (2000). Keeping the peace: Police discretion and mentally ill persons. *National Institute of Justice Journal, 244,* 8-15.

Teplin, L. A., McClelland, G. M., Abram, K. M., and Weiner, D. A. (2005). Crime victimization in adults with severe mental illness: Comparison with the National Crime Victimization Survey. *Archives of General Psychiatry, 62*(8), 911-921.

Tucker, A. S., Van Hasselt, V. B., and Russell, S. A. (2008). Law enforcement response to the mentally ill: An evaluative review. *Brief Treatment and Crisis Intervention, 8*(3), 236.

Vermette, H. S., Pinals, D. A., and Appelbaum, P. S. (2005). Mental health training for law enforcement professionals. *Journal of the American Academy of Psychiatry and the Law Online, 33*(1), 42-46.

Watson, A. C., Corrigan, P. W., and Ottati, V. (2004). Police officers' attitudes toward and decisions about persons with mental illness. *Psychiatric Services, 55*(1), 49-53.

Wells, W., and Schafer, J. A. (2006). Officer perceptions of police responses to persons with a mental illness. *Policing: An International Journal of Police Strategies and Management, 29*(4), 578-601.

A.4

MENTAL HEALTH IN LATIN AMERICA AND THE CARIBBEAN

Dévora Kestel, M.Sc.
Pan American Health Organization

"There is no health without mental health." Despite this powerful statement, the mental health situation in Latin America and Caribbean countries (LAC) still lags behind where it should and could be. To analyze this situation from a public health perspective, we have selected a few indicators that facilitate the comparison among countries and sub-regions, and that at the same time provide sufficient information to adequately understand the current situation and appreciate potential opportunities from a regional perspective.

Although the general data available from LAC present a situation that could be viewed as dismal, it is important to highlight that there are many good examples in the region worth replicating. There are countries that have been reforming—a continuously ongoing process—their mental health system for decades; there are also regions or towns within countries that use their autonomy to move the mental health agenda forward, even when the national situation is not as advanced.

This brief article intends to highlight some of the most salient features of mental health systems in LAC.

Burden, Prevalence, and Treatment Gap

Recent studies of the global burden of disease show once again the importance of considering mental health as a public health issue (1). Depression is the eleventh cause of disability globally (before TB, diabetes, and lung cancer), and it ranks from third to seventh in the Americas region, depending on the different subregions being considered (2).

Noncommunicable diseases (NCDs) account for 54 percent of the total global health burden, and mental health and substance use disorders and are the biggest contributors to the NCD burden. In LAC, the Disability Adjusted Life Years due to neuropsychiatric disorders amount to 14 percent of the total amount (11 percent mental and behavioral disorders, 3 percent intentional injuries) (1).

Comparing the prevalence of these disorders with the available records of attendance to mental health services allows for the identification of a treatment gap. A treatment gap represents the percentage of people with severe mental disorders that do not receive treatment (3). At the global level, data from 2004 showed the extent of the treatment gap: 35.5 to 50.3 percent of serious cases did not receive any treatment within the prior year in developed countries, but the proportion of cases not receiving any treatment in developing countries was much higher: 76 to 85 percent. These figures clearly indicate how the problem of mental health services availability is not just of concern in developing countries (4).

A recent study of the treatment gap in LAC highlights that 73.5 percent of adults with severe and moderate affective disorders, anxiety disorders, and substance use disorders in the Americas do not receive treatment (47.2 percent in North America, and 77.9 percent in LAC). In the United States, the treatment gap for schizophrenia is 42.0 percent, and in LAC, 56.2 percent (5).

Resources Availability

One partial explanation for this significant gap is the inadequacy of funds available to develop appropriate services for those suffering from mental and neurological disorders. The world median of the health budget allocated to mental health is 2.82 percent (6).

Mental health expenditures at the regional level are not that different from global levels; the median health budget allocated to mental health is 2.3 percent, with differences linked to sub-regional characteristics.

In the context of the existing limited budget environment, it is very important to understand how those resources are used. The principal part of that budget goes to outdated, custodial style, psychiatric hospitals, with very limited funds made available for the development of community-based mental health services. Specifically, in the English-speaking Caribbean countries, the mental health budget is 3.5 percent of the health budget, and 84 percent of that budget goes to mental hospitals. In Central America, the mental health budget is even lower, at 1.5 percent of the health budget, with 75 percent of it spent in mental hospitals. In South America, the budget represents 2 percent of the health budget, with 66 percent going to mental hospitals (7).

Figure A-1 illustrates the median percentage of the government health budget allocated to mental health and to psychiatric hospitals, by subregion and total.

Policies, Plans, and Laws in Mental Health

Having a mental health policy and or a plan (whether it is independent or integrated as part of a general health document is not relevant) is very important to concentrate efforts and available resources into common objectives that will lead to a positive impact on the mental health of the population.

Most of the countries and territories in the region have developed mental health policies and plans; only six of them still do not have such a policy tool. However, having a document written and approved does not necessarily mean that it is being implemented. Several countries have a newly developed mental health policy or plan that advocates for the development of community-based mental health services, while, for example, their services remain concentrated in mental hospitals (7).

Regarding mental health legislation, only eight countries have legislation specific for mental health issued after the year 2000. The implications in this context are related to the lack of appropriate instruments to protect and promote the human rights of the mentally ill and their families.

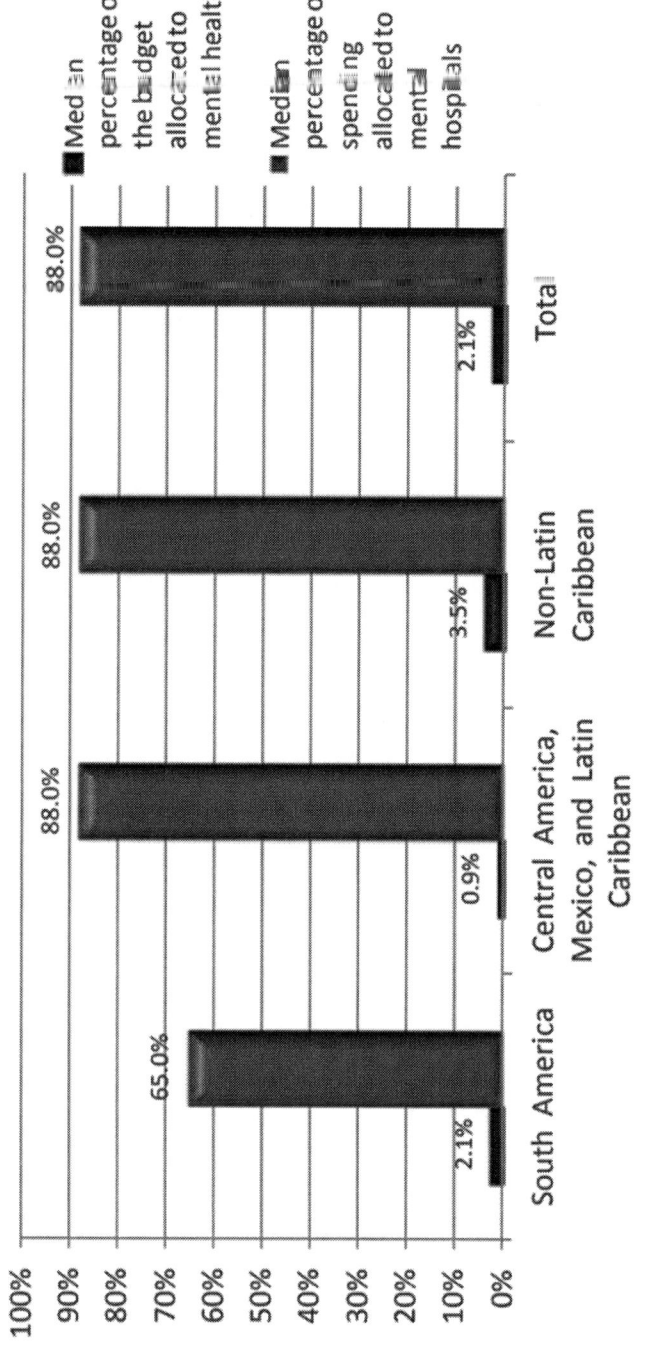

FIGURE A-1 Mental health expenditures (7).
SOURCE: Figure developed by Dévora Kestel for the WHO-AIMS: Report on Mental Health Systems in Latin America and the Caribbean, by Dévora Kestel, copyright 2013 PAHO. Reprinted with the permission of the Pan American Health Organization.

Mental Health Professionals

Broadly speaking about human resources, there is limited availability of personnel working in mental health. At the global level, there is less than one psychiatrist per 200,000 people or more.

In the LAC region, there are 2.1 psychiatrists per 100,000 people. Although the national average in some countries may not necessarily be small, most of them are frequently concentrated in the capital or main cities of the country, leaving large territories uncovered. Other mental health professionals are generally less present in the region. The presence of nurses, psychologists (with the exception of some countries in South America), social workers, and occupational therapists is quite limited, ranging from around two to less than one professional of each category per 100,000 inhabitants.

Table A-1 below offers a summary of mental health workers available in the LAC region (7).

Organization of Mental Health Services

The analysis of existing services in LAC highlights the inefficiency in the location of beds. Globally, 62 percent of psychiatric beds are located in mental hospitals, with 21 percent in general hospitals, and just 16 percent in residential facilities (6, 7).

TABLE A-1 Mental Health Professionals in LAC

Subregion	Psychiatrists	Nurses	Psychologists	Social Workers	Occupational Therapists	Others
Central America, Mexico and Latin Caribbean	1.5	2.3	2	0.7	0.2	2.3
Non-Latin Caribbean	1.9	14.3*	0.3	1.1	0.1	20.8
South America	2.9	1.6	10.2	1.1	0.2	3.8
Total average	2.1	6	4.2	1	0.2	9

* A few islands with a small population and a relatively high number of general nurses (all involved with mental health patients) create this high number.
SOURCE: Presented by Dévora Kestel on October 30, 2015.

In LAC, 86.6 percent of the total number of available psychiatric beds are located in psychiatric hospitals, meaning that in many countries, the only answer for people suffering from mental disorders is a bed in a psychiatric hospital, which, in the majority of cases, are outdated custodial institutions that promote a systematic violation of human rights (7).

If a person is in need of hospitalization for an acute episode, he or she would have to access one of the 10.6 percent of the total number of available beds located in general hospitals that are dedicated to psychiatric care (7).

For those persons who may need a longer time to recover without necessarily needing hospital care, they should be considered lucky to access the limited number of beds available in residential facilities (2.7 percent of the total number of available beds) (7).

Paradoxically, when looking at the flow of patients in different mental health facilities, results indicate that those same hospitals that concentrate most of the limited available resources deal with between 5 and 13 percent of the total number of patients who visit any mental health facility in the year assessed. (7) The rest of the patients are seen by ambulatory services, in general hospitals, or in any other service available at the community level, developed with only 12 percent of the budget available for mental health (as mentioned above, 88 percent of the budget dedicated to mental health goes to traditional mental hospitals).

Table A-2 illustrates the number of mental health services' users, by 100,000 people, visiting available facilities in the year of World Health Organization Assessment Instrument for Mental Health Systems (WHO-AIMS)

TABLE A-2 Number of Users Attending Mental Health Facilities

Subregion	Outpatient Facilities (median)	Day Hospitals	Psychiatric Units in General Hospitals	Residential Facilities	Psychiatric Hospitals
South America	1.232	22.3	83.3	4.7	70.72
Central America, Mexico and Latin Caribbean	588	5.1	50	0.6	68
Non-Latin Caribbean	936	7.5	119	2.5	171.4

SOURCE: Presented by Dévora Kestel on October 30, 2015.

implementation in their respective country. Although the data collection is not precise (sometimes miscounting a patient with a contact), it nevertheless offers an idea of the patient flow. For instance, looking at South America, 70.72 patients were treated in psychiatric hospitals, while over a thousand were treated in all other services available and developed with very limited resources (7).

Good Experiences in the Region

In 1990, a regional Conference for Restructuring of Psychiatric Care was held in Caracas, Venezuela. That conference is considered to be an important milestone in the region because of its recognition of the need to move the attention, until then primarily focused on the psychiatric hospital, to the development of decentralized, community-based services that are participatory, comprehensive, and that ensure continuity of care. The conference also introduced the need to ensure the protection of patients' human rights.

Since then, several regional declarations paired with Pan American Health Organization (PAHO) and WHO resolutions have been expanded and approved by member states, all of which aim at the development of a mental health system that will eventually provide an appropriate answer to the mental health needs of the population.

In parallel, several countries in the region are at different stages of serious reforms to their mental health systems, in some cases at the national level, and in others at the regional or even local level.

In October 2013, the World Health Assembly approved a Comprehensive Mental Health Plan of Action that emphasized the need to move ahead in this path that was initiated several years or decades ago (8).

In 2014, PAHO prepared an update to its Regional Mental Health Plan of Action to align it with the global plan. The regional plan is expected to be approved by the Ministers of Health of the Americas by October 2014.

The priorities identified in these plans are concentrated around four main areas:

- Leadership and governance
- Community-based mental health and social care services
- Promotion and prevention
- Information systems, evidence, and research

The adaptation of these plans to national realities should help countries move ahead with needed reforms to their existing mental health services.

Final Considerations

Although countries are moving toward the development of community-based mental health services that are decentralized and closer to people's realities, there is still much to do to have the region ready to answer to situations related to violence or other specific needs, such as the appropriate response to populations affected by disasters (natural or man-made) and the needs of vulnerable groups.

Countries in the region will be ready to answer to these situations when an appropriate range of mental health services, from promotion and prevention to rehabilitation and recovery, based in the community will be available and when mental health will fully be integrated with general health services.

When discussing violence and mental health, mental health professionals should be aware that most LACs' mental health systems create and direct violence toward individuals with mental disorders and their families. Until changes occur to their mental health systems, this violence will continue to neglect to provide patients with the attention and services they need and will maintain the idea that the mentally ill are violent.

Integrating mental health with general health services is a good strategy to ensure that the health system as a whole will offer adequate care to the people who need it.

References

1. Murray, C. J. L. et al. Disability-adjusted life years (DALYs) for 291 diseases and injuries in 21 regions, 1990–2010: A systematic analysis for the Global Burden of Disease Study. 2010. *Lancet*, 2012; 380: 2197–2223.
2. Ferrari, A. J., Charlson, F. J., Norman, R. E., Patten, S. B., Freedman G., et al. 2013. Burden of depressive disorders by country, sex, age and year: Findings from the Global Burden of Disease Study 2010. *PLoS Med* 10(11): e1001547. doi: 10.1371/journal.pmed.1001547.
3. Kohn, R., Saxena, S., Levav, I., and Saraceno, B. 2004. The treatment gap in mental health care. *Bull World Health Organ* 82: 858-66 pmid: 15640922.
4. World Health Organization. World Mental Health Survey Consortium. 2004. Prevalence, severity, and unmet need for treatment of mental disorders in the World Health Organization World Mental Health Surveys. *JAVA*, http://www.ncbi.nlm.nih.gov/pubmed/15173149.
5. Kohn, R. 2013. *Treatment gap in the Americas*, http://www.paho.org/hq/index.php?option=com_contentandview=articleandid=9408andItemid=99999.
6. World Health Organization. 2011. Mental Health ATLAS 2011, http://www.who.int/mental_health/publications/mental_health_atlas_2011/en.
7. Pan American Health Organization. 2013. *WHO-AIMS: Report on mental health systems in Latin America and the Caribbean*, http://www.paho.org/hq/index.php?option=com_contentandview=articleandid=935andItemid=1106andlang=enandlimitstart=7.
8. World Health Organization. *Comprehensive mental health action plan 2013–2020*, http://www.who.int/mental_health/publications/action_plan/en.

A.5

HEAVY EPISODIC ALCOHOL USE AND INTIMATE PARTNER VIOLENCE: A CROSS-CULTURAL PUBLIC HEALTH ISSUE

Cory A. Crane, Ph.D.
Kenneth E. Leonard, Ph.D.

Research Institute on Addictions
University at Buffalo

Intimate partner violence (IPV) involves the perpetration of physically aggressive acts against a spouse or dating partner and has been identified as a serious social concern with considerable health and financial costs at the individual, family, and societal levels (Lawrence et al., 2012). A review of 249 peer-reviewed articles detected a high prevalence of past year and lifetime (19.2 percent and 33.6 percent, respectively) physical IPV victimization among heterosexual individuals, with slightly higher rates of victimization among females (23.1 percent) than males (19.1 percent) across all studies (Desmarais et al., 2012). In a separate review of 111 articles, Desmarais and colleagues (2012) reported comparable rates of physical IPV perpetration across all participants (24.8 percent) with slightly higher rates of female-to-male (28.3 percent) than male-to-female (21.6 percent) perpetration.

Traditional conceptual models of IPV focused on constructs such as gender roles, power and control, and cultural sanctions for male-to-female aggression, and were advanced through a societal mandate to help explain and prevent IPV (Pence and Paymar, 1993). These early models spawned intervention approaches and public policies that focused on accountability as well as psychoeducation and remain predominant today (Babcock et al., 2004). Those who adhered to this early conceptual framework argued that alcohol use should be considered an unacceptable excuse for violent behavior and unequivocally rejected the notion that intoxication may play a causal role in episodes of IPV. The past 20 years of research, however, has largely failed to support both the traditional models (Dutton and Corvo, 2007) and associated interventions (Babcock et al., 2004), and has offered largely consistent empirical support for an alternative conceptualization of heavy alcohol use as a contributing causal factor in episodes of IPV (Leonard, 2005).

This research has been guided by and has contributed to the current prevailing theories describing the proximal effects of heavy alcohol consumption on violent behavior, which focus on attention allocation and the disinhibiting characteristics of alcohol. These theories are based on the direct psychopharmacological effects of alcohol, which include a wide range of transitory impairments in higher-order executive cognitive functioning (Giancola et al., 2010). Among other effects, alcohol intoxication is thought to impair decision making through the exacerbation or amplification of attention to dominant environmental cues that may instigate violence while limiting attention to less salient cues that may inhibit violent responding, such as the long-term consequences of violent actions (Steele and Josephs, 1990; Taylor and Leonard, 1983). Alcohol expectancies serve as the basis for an alternative set of theories by which alcohol facilitates IPV through the perpetrator's own beliefs about the mitigating effects of intoxication on one's own culpability for socially unacceptable partner violent behavior. Although alcohol expectancy theories have received some scientific support, the majority of research has found little evidence for moderating effects on the relationship between alcohol intoxication and the perpetration of partner violence (e.g., Quigley and Leonard, 2006).

Human research contributing to our current understanding of the relationship between heavy alcohol use and IPV has utilized survey, longitudinal, event-based, experimental, and treatment-evaluation methodologies to support an assertion of causality based on the preponderance of evidence drawn from the multi-method approach (Leonard, 2005). Prior reviews have detected a significant effect of alcohol on general physical aggression (e.g., $d = .22$; Lipsey et al., 1997) and provided further empirical impetus to extend this work into the field of partner violence, resulting in multiple meta-analytic investigations examining the relationship between indices of heavy alcohol use and IPV within cross-sectional and case control studies, inclusive of considerable diversity in sample characteristics. These reviews find high heterogeneity across studies and significant overall effect sizes in the small to medium range. Ferrer and colleagues (2004) examined 9 studies and reported that male IPV perpetrators were more likely to abuse or be dependent upon alcohol than non-violent male participants ($d = .57$). Stith and colleagues (2004) reached similar conclusions regarding the effect size of alcohol on IPV perpetration after aggregating data from 22 studies of male participants ($d = .48$).

In an effort to update prior reviews and examine moderators that may account for the heterogeneity in effect sizes across studies reported in previous meta-analyses, Foran and O'Leary (2008) conducted the most recent and comprehensive review of this literature. In addition to corroborating the small-to-medium relationship between alcohol and IPV among males ($d = .47$), a small but tentatively homogeneous relationship was detected among eight studies involving female participants ($d = .28$). Moderation analyses examined the robustness of effects across various male sample characteristics. Effects did not differ across married and dating samples.

The relationship between alcohol and IPV was comparable across clinical and community samples as well. Not included in moderation analyses, the small-to-medium relationship between heavy alcohol use and IPV has been reported within incarcerated (e.g., Logan et al., 2001; White et al., 2001), emergency department (Lipsky et al., 2005), and military (Pan et al., 1994) samples, and nascent literature indicates an association among gay and lesbian samples, as well (Klostermann et al., 2011). Furthermore, research indicates that the link between heavy alcohol use and IPV is a cross-cultural phenomenon extending across ethnic groups (Caetano et al., 2001) and beyond Western nations with varying alcohol use and violence norms, including countries in South America (Kishor and Johnson, 2004), Asia (Rao, 1997), and Africa (Yigzaw et al., 2005). Most recently, problematic male alcohol use was determined to increase the odds of male-to-female IPV perpetration in 12 of 14 regions (N = 24,097 across 10 countries) that participated in the World Health Organization Multi-Country Study on Women's Health and Domestic Violence population-based survey study between the years of 2000 and 2003 (Abramsky et al., 2011). Thus, the existing literature provides consistent evidence for an association between heavy alcohol use and IPV that can be observed widely.

There have been fewer longitudinal investigations addressing the association between heavy alcohol use and IPV. However, the available evidence suggests that heavy alcohol use is longitudinally predictive of IPV perpetration over short follow-up periods, but the evidence is less supportive over long follow-up periods. Although not a longitudinal study, Leonard et al. (1985) found that alcohol disorders within the past 3 years were predictive of husband IPV, while alcohol disorders that occurred before the last 3 years were not. This observation is consistent with longitudinal research involving premarital (Heyman et al., 1995) and newlywed (Quigley and Leonard, 1999) couples in which alcohol problems were predictive of IPV at the earliest, but not subsequent, follow-ups. Leonard and Senchack (1996) reported that prospective reports of premarital problematic alcohol use were predictive of physical IPV perpetration among husbands during the subsequent first year of marriage, even after controlling for premarital IPV. Similarly, Keller and colleagues (2009) reported that husband, but not wife, alcohol problems predicted increased physical IPV at a 2-year follow-up. The composite longitudinal evidence indicates that problematic alcohol use may be longitudinally associated with subsequent IPV and that this relationship may attenuate over time, possibly in response to shifting patterns of alcohol use as well as dynamic dyadic coping and adjustment strategies.

These studies demonstrate a general association between alcohol and IPV, but lack the temporal element necessary to establish causation. This proximal relationship can be best established through event-based as well as laboratory analogue or experimental methodologies. Event-based research reveals that alcohol is often involved in IPV events and that perpetrator intoxication is predictive of both the occurrence and severity of violence. On the international scale, a cross-sectional study of the most severe episodes of physical IPV experienced by male and female respondents in 13 nations revealed relative uniformity in greater violence severity among alcohol-involved events compared to sober events (Graham et al., 2011). In the United States, an examination of epidemiological data provided by a subset of male (n = 501) and female (n = 1,756) participants who reported IPV victimization on the National Violence Against Women Survey (NVAWS; Tjaden and Thoennes, 2000) demonstrated that 33.6 percent of IPV events involved perpetrators under the influence of alcohol and that, after controlling for victim alcohol use, females were more likely to sustain injuries if their male partner had been drinking heavily (Thompson and Kingree, 2006).

Past year conflict interviews of 366 newlywed couples were conducted at their first wedding anniversary and similarly revealed that husbands were more likely to be drinking during physically, rather than verbally, violent conflicts (Leonard and Quigley, 1999). Participants from 61 of these couples completed conflict interviews after the third anniversary and described both an alcohol-involved and a non-alcohol-involved IPV episode (Testa et al., 2003). Episodes of IPV in which the husband reported alcohol use evidenced more violent acts, more severe violence, and greater mutual violence than episodes that did not involve husband alcohol use. High rates of perpetrator alcohol use during IPV events have also been reported by victims in emergency departments (Lipsky et al., 2005) and higher blood alcohol levels have been reported during violent conflicts in comparison to nonviolent conflicts by treatment-seeking alcoholics (Murphy et al., 2005). At the greatest extreme, proxy and victim reports reveal that rates of problematic drinking may be even higher among intimate partner homicide perpetrators (52.0 percent) than nonfatal partner violence perpetrators (30.9 percent) and that the majority of intimate partner homicides (59.5 percent) may occur while the perpetrator is under the influence of alcohol (Campbell et al., 2003; Sharps et al., 2001).

Prospective research techniques (e.g., daily diary and ecological momentary assessment) represent an amalgam of longitudinal and event-based methodologies and allow for a daily process analysis of the relationship between heavy alcohol use and IPV through frequent reporting. A single, recent investigation collected 56 independent, daily reports from both members of 118 community couples (Testa and Derrick, 2014). Despite detecting expectedly few acts of IPV during the study period, perpetrator alcohol use significantly predicted subsequent physical IPV perpetration both later in the same day and within 4 hours.

These types of observational designs provide strong evidence for correlations between heavy alcohol use and IPV but retrospective, self-reported accounts of alcohol-involved IPV are subject to recall errors and other reporting biases. Although previous meta-analyses have intentionally excluded the experimental literature (e.g., Foran and O'Leary, 2008), a number of carefully controlled experimental studies have examined the direct effects of alcohol administration on proxy measures of IPV and remain integral to establishing the case for causality under the most rigorous criteria. The sexual (for a review, see Abbey, 2011; Rehm et al., 2012) and general (for a review, see Exum, 2006) aggression literatures are replete with examples of experimental evidence supporting the effects of heavy alcohol consumption on aggressive and violent responding, such as setting more frequent or intense shocks for an opponent after having received alcohol in a competitive reaction time task (Bushman, 1997). The ecological validity of traditional aggression paradigms to IPV perpetration has been called into question, necessitating the generation of contemporary assessment methodologies that more closely approximate relationship-specific stressors, instigators, and aggressive response options (Tedeschi and Quigley, 1996).

Conflict resolution studies recruit couples to identify and discuss sources of relationship conflict with active alcohol manipulations. Coding of these recorded conversations has revealed effects of alcohol on IPV-related verbal behaviors. In a sample of 145 newlywed couples, Leonard and Roberts (1998) reported that husbands who had received alcohol, as well as their sober wives, displayed greater verbal negativity than those couples in which the husband had received either a placebo or nonalcoholic beverage. Similar effects of acute alcohol consumption on negativity during couple interactions have been detected among alcohol-abusing participants (Haber and Jacob, 1997; Jacob and Krahn, 1988; Jacob and Leonard, 1988). Other research has demonstrated that the effects of alcohol on negativity among alcohol abusing husbands may be confined to those with high antisocial tendencies (Jacob et al., 2001). A recent study (Testa et al., 2014) offered discrepant findings, detecting no negative effects of a couple's alcohol manipulation on relationship interactions. The couples in this study were unique, however, in that they reported relatively high relationship satisfaction, were involved in stable long-term relationships, and were both heavy social drinkers, suggesting that they had likely developed satisfactory skills to cope with alcohol-involved conflict.

An alternative experimental paradigm involves recoding verbal responses to audio situations involving a simulated intimate partner. Examination of response content for aggressive intent consistently reveals that participants react with greater aggression following alcohol administration and anger induction. Eckhardt (2007) randomly assigned a sample of 102 husbands to an alcohol, placebo, or nonalcoholic beverage condition and reported the greatest aggressive verbalizations among the participants who received alcohol, particularly if they had reported previously perpetrating marital violence. Using the same paradigm, Eckhardt and Crane (2008) detected a comparable effect of alcohol on aggressive verbalizations among a sample of 37 male and 33 female participants, particularly among those who reported high dispositional aggressive responding.

The research detailed above strongly supports alcohol as a contributing cause to IPV. Heavy or problematic alcohol use at the time of IPV perpetration does not function as a unilateral determinant of IPV, however, as evidenced by small-to-medium effect sizes and high heterogeneity across meta-analyses, IPV episodes that involve no alcohol in event-based studies, as well as variability across individuals in experimental data. Emerging from the aforementioned disinhibition and attention allocation models, individual and situational factors may increase the likelihood of alcohol-involved IPV. Indeed, individuals with low relationship satisfaction (e.g., Leonard and Senchak, 1996), high dispositional anger (e.g., Norlander and Eckhardt, 2005), aggressive tendencies (e.g., Eckhardt and Crane, 2008), and antisociality (e.g., Leonard and Senchak, 1996) seem to be at high risk of IPV perpetration following heavy alcohol consumption. Similarly, longitudinal data suggest that alcohol problems are associated with increased IPV perpetration the following year only among husbands high in both hostility and avoidance coping strategies (Schumacher et al., 2008). However, as noted by Leonard (2005), there is evidence to suggest that this synergistic effect breaks down among the most highly aggressive, and that for these individuals, alcohol may increase the severity of aggression, but not the occurrence. This notion, which came to be referred to as the "Multiple Thresholds" theory, has been explicated by Fals-Stewart, Leonard, and Birchler (2005).

Treatment

It is important to recognize that alcohol is neither a necessary nor a sufficient cause of intimate partner violence but instead, it contributes, in concert with other factors, to an increase in the occurrence and severity of such violence. Hence, in some groups, alcohol may have a minimal impact on IPV, while in other groups, its impact may be quite substantial. This is most apparent when we examine treatment populations. These populations offer a unique opportunity to observe both the association between problematic alcohol use and IPV as well as mutual changes in these conditions over time. We see strikingly high rates of comorbidity regardless of the identified treatment sample. Alcohol problems are detected in upwards of 50 percent of mandated and voluntary male IPV treatment seekers (e.g., Brown et al., 1999; Dalton, 2001; Gondolf, 1999; Stuart, et al., 2003).

High rates of hazardous drinking are also detected among female IPV offenders (Stuart et al., 2003). Rates of IPV among substance abuse treatment seeking samples also routinely exceed 50 percent in both male and female samples (e.g., Chase et al., 2003; Gondolf and Foster, 1991; Murphy and O'Farrell, 1994; Murphy et al., 2001).

Despite the high co-occurrence of problematic alcohol use and IPV, the behaviors are not routinely assessed unless included among the initial referral questions (Easton et al., 2007). Little evidence supports the effectiveness of IPV treatment programs at preventing subsequent acts of violence. Meta-analytic reviews have revealed small or non-significant effects, suggesting that treatment may reduce the risk of IPV by as little as 5 percent beyond legal intervention alone (e.g., Babcock et al., 2004; Feder and Wilson, 2005). Eckhardt and colleagues (2013) recently collected all case controlled studies of IPV treatment programs to report that the existing research, though methodologically flawed, contained roughly equivocal support for and against the effectiveness of IPV interventions. The failure of IPV treatment programs has been attributed, in part, to poor rates of attendance and high attrition (Babcock and Steiner, 1999; Gondolf, 2000). Heavy alcohol use may also impact the poor outcomes of IPV treatment inasmuch as IPV perpetrators with alcohol problems attend fewer sessions and drop out of treatment at a greater rate than perpetrators without drinking problems (for a review, see Daly and Pelowski, 2000; Olver et al., 2011).

Indeed, substance abuse treatment success has been associated with reductions in IPV. One investigation found that intensive treatment for alcohol dependence, in the absence of IPV-specific content, resulted in significant reductions not only in alcohol use but also physical and psychological IPV perpetration at 6- and 12-month follow-ups, according to male clients and their wives (Stuart et al., 2003). Similar results were found among a sample of females seeking treatment for alcohol dependence; treatment resulted in reductions in alcohol, physical violence, and psychological IPV perpetration at 6- and 12-month follow ups (Stuart et al., 2002). In a larger treatment evaluation study, alcohol treatment resulted in reductions in the prevalence of IPV from baseline assessment to 1-year follow-up and a greater increase in IPV among relapsed clients relative to remitted clients at 2 year follow-up (O'Farrell et al., 2003).

When detected, however, dual alcohol problems and IPV most often result in assignment to separate treatment programs that fail to coordinate efforts to minimize client burden, reducing the likelihood of completing either program (Bennett and Lawson, 1994; Schumacher et al., 2003). Initial evidence suggests that integrated alcohol and IPV treatments may be more effective than treatment as usual. Evaluations of behavioral couples therapy for alcohol and IPV problems have evidenced reductions in alcohol use as well as the prevalence of IPV among both male and female partners at a 1-year follow-up, again with less violence among remitted compared to relapsed clients (O'Farrell et al., 2000; O'Farrell et al., 2004). A separate investigation reported significant reductions in IPV from baseline to post-treatment among clients randomly assigned to an integrated cognitive-behavioral therapy for substance abuse and IPV but not clients assigned to an alternative, standard treatment protocol (Easton et al., 2007).

Thus, research among treatment-seeking samples offers further confirmation of the general interrelationship between alcohol and IPV while highlighting the need to address both conditions among relevant clinical samples. Problematic alcohol use is associated with IPV treatment dropout, and successful substance abuse treatment reduces the risk of future IPV perpetration beyond violence interventions alone. Even still, integrated programs for clients with special treatment needs are routinely met with resistance and remain more the exception than the norm.

Future Directions

Although we have briefly reviewed the literature that has contributed to our considerable understanding of the effects of acute heavy alcohol consumption on IPV, there is a dearth of research into the effects of chronic heavy alcohol use on the risk of perpetrating IPV. The processes by which chronic heavy alcohol consumption may affect the ability to interpret and select prosocial responses to incoming social stimuli remain unclear. One model describes indirect effects, positing that chronic alcohol use increases the risk of IPV through gradual changes to interpersonal dynamics that reduce relationship satisfaction, increase relationship stress, and decrease reliance upon non-violent conflict resolution tactics designed to accommodate a partner or improve the partnership (Quigley and Leonard, 1999). Alternatively, neurobiological evidence reveals that chronic alcohol use is associated with neuronal death and widespread deficits in executive cognitive functioning (e.g., Sullivan et al., 2002). Easton and colleagues (2008) extended this research to report greater cognitive impairment (e.g., attention, concentration, flexibility) among alcohol-dependent men who reported IPV perpetration when compared to alcohol-dependent men who reported no IPV perpetration. As previously stated, much of the existing research provides evidence for the proximal effects of heavy alcohol consumption on IPV, even among individuals with chronic alcohol abuse problems. Additional long-term longitudinal and neuropsychological research beginning in adolescence and extending through early adulthood is required to further develop our understanding of the biopsychosocial effects of chronic alcohol use on IPV.

The role of psychopathology, as well as its interaction with alcohol, in IPV perpetration represents another underdeveloped area of research. Similar to alcohol, early IPV models conceptualized mental illness as an excuse for unacceptable violence (Pence and Paymar, 1993). Although emerging research now suggests that certain mental health conditions associated with impulse control problems or affective dysregulation, such as mood and anxiety disorders, may increase the risk of IPV perpetration (Crane et al., 2014; Hatters-Friedman and Loue, 2007), existing IPV treatment protocols fail to take mental illness into consideration. Given initial evidence that suggests a synergistic effect of substance use and mental illness on violent behavior (e.g., Van Dorn et al., 2012), the effects of mental illness on compliance and recidivism may need to be evaluated within the context of IPV treatment and existing interventions adapted to improve outcomes for this select group as well as their partners.

Our review of IPV treatment research suggests that current options are insufficient to accomplish the goal of violence prevention and that there is a great need for the development and evaluation of more effective interventions that focus on individual needs rather than a uniform protocol. Heavy alcohol consumption, as a contributing cause of IPV, and interactions between alcohol use and partner influences are emerging as important treatment considerations. As such, nascent research into integrated treatment programs for both problematic alcohol use and IPV show promise, as do relationship-systems interventions that focus on dynamic, interactive processes at the couple level. The available treatment portfolio and public policies that govern their implementation must be expanded to accommodate individual substance use, psychiatric, and dyadic needs.

References

Abbey, A. (2011). Alcohol's role in sexual violence perpetration: Theoretical explanations, existing evidence and future directions. *Drug and Alcohol Review, 30,* 481-489.

Abramsky, T., Watts, C. H., Garcia-Moreno, C., Devries, K., Kiss, L., Ellsberg, M., Hansen, H. A., and Heise, L. (2011). What factors are associated with recent intimate partner violence? Findings from the WHO multi-country study on women's health and domestic violence. *BMC Public Health, 11,* 109-125.

Babcock, J. C., Green, C. E., and Robie, C. (2004). Does batterers' treatment work? A meta-analytic review of domestic violence treatment. *Clinical Psychology Review, 23,* 1023-1053.

Babcock, J. C., and Steiner, R. (1999). The relationship between treatment, incarceration, and recidivism of battering: A program evaluation of Seattle's coordinated community response to domestic violence. *Journal of Family Psychology, 13,* 46-59.

Bennett, L., and Lawson, M. (1994). Barriers to cooperation between domestic-violence and substance-abuse programs. *Families in Society, 75,* 277-286.

Brown, T. G., Werk, A., Caplan, T., and Seraganian, P. (1999). Violent substance abusers in domestic violence treatment. *Violence and Victims, 14,* 179-190.

Bushman, B. J. (1997). Effects of alcohol on human aggression. Validity of proposed explanations. *Recent Developments in Alcoholism, 13,* 227-243.

Caetano, R., Schafer, J., and Cunradi, C. B. (2001). Alcohol-related intimate partner violence among White, Black, and Hispanic couples in the United States. *Alcohol Research and Health, 25,* 58-65.

Campbell, J. C., Webster, D., Koziol-McLain, J., Block, C., Campbell, D., Curry, M. A., ... and Laughon, K. (2003). Risk factors for femicide in abusive relationships: Results from a multisite case control study. *American Journal of Public Health, 93,* 1089-1097.

Chase, K. A., O'Farrell, T. J., Murphy, C. M., Fals-Stewart, W., and Murphy, M. (2003). Factors associated with partner violence among female alcoholic patients and their male partners. *Journal of Studies on Alcohol and Drugs, 64,* 137-149.

Crane, C. A., Hawes, S. W., Devine, S., and Easton, C. J. (2014). Axis I psychopathology and the perpetration of intimate partner violence. *Journal of Clinical Psychology, 70,* 238-247.

Dalton, B. (2001). Batterer characteristics and treatment completion. *Journal of Interpersonal Violence, 16,* 1223-1238.

Daly, J. E., and Pelowski, S. (2000). Predictors of dropout among men who batter: A review of studies with implications for research and practice. *Violence and Victims, 15,* 137-160.

Desmarais, S. L., Reeves, K. A., Nicholls, T. L., Telford, R. P., and Fiebert, M. S. (2012). Prevalence of physical violence in intimate relationships, part 2: Rates of male and female perpetration. *Partner Abuse, 3,* 170-198.

Dutton, D. G., and Corvo, K. (2007). The Duluth Model: A data-impervious paradigm and a failed strategy. *Aggression and Violent Behavior, 12,* 658-667.

Easton, C. J., Mandel, D. L., Hunkele, K. A., Nich, C., Rounsaville, B. J., and Carroll, K. M. (2007). A cognitive behavioral therapy for alcohol-dependent domestic violence offenders: An integrated Substance Abuse–Domestic Violence treatment approach (SADV). *The American Journal on Addictions, 16,* 24-31.

Easton, C. J., Sacco, K. A., Neavins, T. M., Wupperman, P., and George, T. P. (2008). Neurocognitive performance among alcohol dependent men with and without physical violence toward their partners: A preliminary report. *The American Journal of Drug and Alcohol Abuse, 34,* 29-37.

Eckhardt, C. I. (2007). Effects of alcohol intoxication on anger experience and expression among partner assaultive men. *Journal of Consulting and Clinical Psychology, 75,* 61-71.

Eckhardt, C. I., and Crane, C. (2008). Effects of alcohol intoxication and aggressivity on aggressive verbalizations during anger arousal. *Aggressive Behavior, 34,* 428-436.

Eckhardt, C. I., Murphy, C. M., Whitaker, D. J., Sprunger, J., Dykstra, R., and Woodard, K. (2013). The effectiveness of intervention programs for perpetrators and victims of intimate partner violence. *Partner Abuse, 4,* 196-231.

Exum, M. L. (2006). Alcohol and aggression: An integration of findings from experimental studies. *Journal of Criminal Justice, 34,* 131-145.

Fals-Stewart, W., Leonard, K. E., and Birchler, G. R. (2005). The occurrence of male-to-female intimate partner violence on days of men's drinking: The moderating effects of antisocial personality disorder. *Journal of Consulting and Clinical Psychology, 73,* 239-248.

Feder, L., and Wilson, D. B. (2005). A meta-analytic review of court-mandated batterer intervention programs: Can courts affect abusers' behavior? *Journal of Experimental Criminology, 1,* 239-262.

Ferrer, V., Bosch, E., Garcia, E., Manassero, M. A., and Gili, M. (2004). Meta-analytic study of differential characteristics between batterers and non-batterers: The case of psychopathology and consumption of alcohol and drugs. *Psykhe, 13,* 141-156.

Foran, H. M., and O'Leary, K. D. (2008). Alcohol and intimate partner violence: A meta-analytic review. *Clinical Psychology Review, 28,* 1222-1234.

Giancola, P. R., Josephs, R. A., Parrott, D. J., and Duke, A. A. (2010). Alcohol myopia revisited clarifying aggression and other acts of disinhibition through a distorted lens. *Perspectives on Psychological Science, 5*, 265-278.

Gondolf, E. W. (1999). A comparison of four batterer intervention systems: Do court referral, program length, and services matter? *Journal of Interpersonal Violence, 14*, 41-61.

Gondolf, E. W. (2000). How batterer program participants avoid reassault. *Violence against Women, 6*, 1204-1222.

Gondolf, E. W., and Foster, R. A. (1991). Wife assault among VA alcohol rehabilitation patients. *Psychiatric Services, 42*, 74-79.

Graham, K., Bernards, S., Wilsnack, S. C., and Gmel, G. (2011). Alcohol may not cause partner violence but it seems to make it worse: A cross national comparison of the relationship between alcohol and severity of partner violence. *Journal of Interpersonal Violence, 26*, 1503-1523.

Haber, J. R., and Jacob, T. (1997). Marital interactions of male versus female alcoholics. *Family Process, 36*, 385-402.

Hatters-Friedman, S. H., and Loue, S. (2007). Incidence and prevalence of intimate partner violence by and against women with severe mental illness. *Journal of Women's Health, 16*, 471-480.

Heyman, R. E., O'Leary, K. D., and Jouriles, E. N. (1995). Alcohol and aggressive personality styles: Potentiators of serious physical aggression against wives? *Journal of Family Psychology, 9*, 44.

Jacob, T., and Krahn, G. L. (1988). Marital interactions of alcoholic couples: Comparison with depressed and nondistressed couples. *Journal of Consulting and Clinical Psychology, 56*, 73-79.

Jacob, T., and Leonard, K. E. (1988). Alcoholic-spouse interaction as a function of alcoholism subtype and alcohol consumption interaction. *Journal of Abnormal Psychology, 97*, 231-237.

Jacob, T., Leonard, K. E., and Randolph Haber, J. (2001). Family interactions of alcoholics as related to alcoholism type and drinking condition. *Alcoholism: Clinical and Experimental Research, 25*, 835-843.

Keller, P. S., El-Sheikh, M., Keiley, M., and Liao, P. (2009). Longitudinal relations between marital aggression and alcohol problems. *Psychology of Addictive Behaviors, 23*, 2-13.

Kishor, S., and Johnson, K. (2004). *Profiling domestic violence: A multi-country study*. Calverton, MD: ORC Macro.

Klostermann, K., Kelley, M. L., Milletich, R. J., and Mignone, T. (2011). Alcoholism and partner aggression among gay and lesbian couples. *Aggression and Violent Behavior, 16*, 115-119.

Lawrence, E., Orengo-Aguayo, R., Langer, A., and Brock, R. L. (2012). The impact and consequences of partner abuse on partners. *Partner Abuse, 3*, 406-428.

Leonard, K. E. (2005). Alcohol and intimate partner violence: When can we say that heavy drinking is a contributing cause of violence? *Addiction, 100*, 422-425.

Leonard, K. E., Bromet, E. J., Parkinson, D. K., Day, N. L., and Ryan, C. M. (1985). Patterns of alcohol use and physically aggressive behavior in men. *Journal of Studies on Alcohol and Drugs, 46*, 279-282.

Leonard, K. E., and Quigley, B. M. (1999). Drinking and marital aggression in newlyweds: An event-based analysis of drinking and the occurrence of husband marital aggression. *Journal of Studies on Alcohol and Drugs, 60*, 537-545.

Leonard, K. E., and Roberts, L. J. (1998). The effects of alcohol on the marital interactions of aggressive and nonaggressive husbands and their wives. *Journal of Abnormal Psychology, 107*, 602-615.

Leonard, K. E., and Senchak, M. (1996). Prospective prediction of husband marital aggression within newlywed couples. *Journal of Abnormal Psychology, 105*, 369-380.

Lipsey, M. W., Wilson, D. B., Cohen, M. A., and Derzon, J. H. (1997). Is there a causal relationship between alcohol use and violence? In M. Galanter (Ed.), *Recent developments in alcoholism: Vol. 13. Alcohol and violence – Epidemiology, neurobiology, psychology, family issues* (First ed., pp. 245-282). Springer: US.

Lipsky, S., Caetano, R., Field, C. A., and Larkin, G. L. (2005). Psychosocial and substance-use risk factors for intimate partner violence. *Drug and Alcohol Dependence, 78*, 39-47.

Logan, T. K., Walker, R., Staton, M., and Leukefeld, C. (2001). Substance use and intimate violence among incarcerated males. *Journal of Family Violence, 16*, 93-114.

Murphy, C. M., and O'Farrell, T. J. (1994). Factors associated with marital aggression in male alcoholics. *Journal of Family Psychology, 8*, 321-335.

Murphy, C. M., O'Farrell, T. J., Fals-Stewart, W., and Feehan, M. (2001). Correlates of intimate partner violence among male alcoholic patients. *Journal of Consulting and Clinical Psychology, 69*, 528-540.

Murphy, C. M., Winters, J., O'Farrell, T. J., Fals-Stewart, W., and Murphy, M. (2005). Alcohol consumption and intimate partner violence by alcoholic men: Comparing violent and nonviolent conflicts. *Psychology of Addictive Behaviors, 19*, 35-42.

Norlander, B., and Eckhardt, C. (2005). Anger, hostility, and male perpetrators of intimate partner violence: A meta-analytic review. *Clinical Psychology Review, 25*, 119-152.

O'Farrell, T. J., Fals-Stewart, W., Murphy, M., and Murphy, C. M. (2003). Partner violence before and after individually based alcoholism treatment for male alcoholic patients. *Journal of Consulting and Clinical Psychology, 71*, 92-102.

O'Farrell, T. J., Murphy, C. M., Neavins, T. M., and Van Hutton, V. (2000). Verbal aggression among male alcoholic patients and their wives in the year before and two years after alcoholism treatment. *Journal of Family Violence, 15*, 295-310.

O'Farrell, T. J., Murphy, C. M., Stephan, S. H., Fals-Stewart, W., and Murphy, M. (2004). Partner violence before and after couples-based alcoholism treatment for male alcoholic patients: The role of treatment involvement and abstinence. *Journal of Consulting and Clinical Psychology, 72*, 202-217.

Olver, M. E., Stockdale, K. C., and Wormith, J. S. (2011). A meta-analysis of predictors of offender treatment attrition and its relationship to recidivism. *Journal of Consulting and Clinical Psychology, 79*, 6-21.

Pan, H. S., Neidig, P. H., and O'Leary, K. D. (1994). Predicting mild and severe husband-to-wife physical aggression. *Journal of Consulting and Clinical Psychology, 62*, 975-981.

Pence, E., and Paymar, M. (1993). *Education groups for men who batter: The Duluth Model*. New York: Springer Publishing Company.

Quigley, B. M., and Leonard, K. E. (1999). Husband alcohol expectancies, drinking, and marital-conflict styles as predictors of severe marital violence among newlywed couples. *Psychology of Addictive Behaviors, 13*, 49-59.

Quigley, B. M., and Leonard, K. E. (2006). Alcohol expectancies and intoxicated aggression. *Aggression and Violent Behavior, 11*, 484-496.

Rao, V. (1997). Wife-beating in rural South India: A qualitative and econometric analysis. *Social Science and Medicine, 44*, 1169-1180.

Rehm, J., Shield, K. D., Joharchi, N., and Shuper, P. A. (2012). Alcohol consumption and the intention to engage in unprotected sex: Systematic review and meta-analysis of experimental studies. *Addiction, 107*, 51-59.

Schumacher, J. A., Fals-Stewart, W., and Leonard, K. E. (2003). Domestic violence treatment referrals for men seeking alcohol treatment. *Journal of Substance Abuse Treatment, 24*, 279-283.

Schumacher, J. A., Homish, G. G., Leonard, K. E., Quigley, B. M., and Kearns-Bodkin, J. N. (2008). Longitudinal moderators of the relationship between excessive drinking and intimate partner violence in the early years of marriage. *Journal of Family Psychology, 22,* 894-904.

Sharps, W., Campbell, J., Campbell, D., Gary, F., and Webster, D. P. (2001). The role of alcohol use in intimate partner femicide. *American Journal on Addictions, 10,* 122-135.

Steele, C. M., and Josephs, R. A. (1990). Alcohol myopia: Its prized and dangerous effects. *American Psychologist, 45,* 921-933.

Stith, S. M., Smith, D. B., Penn, C. E., Ward, D. B., and Tritt, D. (2004). Intimate partner physical abuse perpetration and victimization risk factors: A meta-analytic review. *Aggression and Violent Behavior, 10,* 65-98.

Stuart, G. L., Moore, T. M., Kahler, C. W., and Ramsey, S. E. (2003). Substance abuse and relationship violence among men court-referred to batterers' intervention programs. *Substance Abuse, 24,* 107-122.

Stuart, G. L., Moore, T. M., Ramsey, S. E., and Kahler, C. W. (2003). Relationship aggression and substance use among women court-referred to domestic violence intervention programs. *Addictive Behaviors, 28,* 1603-1610.

Stuart, G. L., Ramsey, S. E., Moore, T. M., Kahler, C. W., Farrell, L. E., Recupero, P. R., and Brown, R. A. (2002). Marital violence victimization and perpetration among women substance abusers: A descriptive study. *Violence Against Women, 8,* 934-952.

Stuart, G. L., Ramsey, S. E., Moore, T. M., Kahler, C. W., Farrell, L. E., Recupero, P. R., and Brown, R. A. (2003). Reductions in marital violence following treatment for alcohol dependence. *Journal of Interpersonal Violence, 18,* 1113-1131.

Sullivan, E. V., Fama, R., Rosenbloom, M. J., and Pfefferbaum, A. (2002). A profile of neuropsychological deficits in alcoholic women. *Neuropsychology, 16,* 74-83.

Taylor, S. P., and Leonard, K. E. (1983). Alcohol and human physical aggression. *Aggression: Theoretical and Empirical Reviews, 2,* 77-101.

Tedeschi, J. T., and Quigley, B. M. (1996). Limitations of laboratory paradigms for studying aggression. *Aggression and Violent Behavior, 1,* 163-177.

Testa, M., Crane, C. A., Quigley, B. M., Levitt, A., and Leonard, K. E. (2014). Effects of administered alcohol on intimate partner interactions in a conflict resolution paradigm. *Journal of Studies on Alcohol and Drugs, 75,* 249-258.

Testa, M., and Derrick, J. L. (2014). A daily process examination of the temporal association between alcohol use and verbal and physical aggression in community couples. *Psychology of Addictive Behaviors, 28,* 127-138.

Testa, M., Quigley, B. M., and Leonard, K. E. (2003). Does alcohol make a difference? Within-participants comparison of incidents of partner violence. *Journal of Interpersonal Violence, 18,* 735-743.

Thompson, M. P., and Kingree, J. B. (2006). The roles of victim and perpetrator alcohol use in intimate partner violence outcomes. *Journal of Interpersonal Violence, 21,* 163-177.

Tjaden, P., and Thoennes, N. (2000). Prevalence and consequences of male-to-female and female-to-male intimate partner violence as measured by the National Violence Against Women Survey. *Violence Against Women, 6,* 142-161.

Van Dorn, R., Volavka, J., and Johnson, N. (2012). Mental disorder and violence: Is there a relationship beyond substance use? *Social Psychiatry and Psychiatric Epidemiology, 47,* 487-503.

White, R. J., Ackerman, R. J., and Caraveo, L. E. (2001). Self-identified alcohol abusers in a low-security federal prison: Characteristics and treatment implications. *International Journal of Offender Therapy and Comparative Criminology, 45,* 214-227.

Yigzaw, T., Yibric, A., and Kebede, Y. (2005). Domestic violence around Gondar in northwest Ethiopia. *Ethiopian Journal of Health Development, 18,* 133-139.

A.6

PEER BULLYING AND MENTAL HEALTH

Dieter Wolke, Ph.D.

*University of Warwick,
Department of Psychology (Lifespan Health and Wellbeing Group) and
Division of Mental Health and Well-being (Warwick Medical School),
Coventry, UK*

This paper considers the importance of bullying as a major risk factor for physical and mental health and adaptation to adult roles, including forming lasting relationships and integrating into work and being economically independent. Evidence is provided that bullying by peers either at school or at home by siblings has been mostly ignored by health professionals but should be considered as a significant risk factor and safeguarding issue. Policy suggestions are made to more effectively recognize and manage affected children.

Bullying

Bullying is the systematic abuse of power and is defined as aggressive behavior or *intentional harm doing* among peers that is carried out *repeatedly*, and involves *an imbalance of power*, either actual or perceived, between the victim and the bully.[1] Bullying can take the form of direct bullying, which includes physical and verbal acts of aggression such as hitting, stealing, name calling, or indirect bullying, which is characterised by social exclusion and rumor spreading.[2,3,4] Children can be involved in bullying as victims and as bullies, but also as bully/victims, a subgroup of victims who display bullying behavior.[5,6] Recently there has been much interest in cyberbullying, which can be broadly defined as any bullying which is performed via electronic means, such as mobile phones or the Internet. Approximately 50 percent of children report having been bullied at some point in their lives, and 10 to 14 percent experience chronic bullying lasting for more than 6 months.[7,8] Between 2 and 5 percent are bullies, and a similar number are bully/victims in childhood/adolescence.[9] Rates of cyberbullying are substantially lower, around 4.5 percent for victims and 2.8 percent for perpetrators (bullies; bully/victims), with up to 90 percent also traditionally (face to face) bullied.[10] Being bullied by peers is the most frequent form of abuse encountered by children, much higher than abuse by parents or other adult perpetrators.[11]

Bullying Is Not a Conduct Disorder

Bullying is found in all societies, including modern hunter–gatherer societies and ancient civilizations. It is considered to be an evolutionary adaptation and the purpose is to gain access to resources, secure survival, reduce stress, and allow for more mating opportunities.[12] Indeed, it has been shown that bullies are highly motivated to gain high status, dominance, and the strategic behavior enables access to social success and romantic partners.[13] Indeed, many bullies of both sexes are bi-strategic, employing both means of bullying but also acts of aggressive "prosocial" behavior to enhance their own position by being public and making the recipient dependent as they cannot reciprocate.[14] Indeed, bullies (but not bully/victims or victims) have been shown to be strong, to have good social and emotional understanding, and to be highly popular.[15] Thus, they are not conduct disordered. Indeed, unlike conduct disorder, bullies are found in all socioeconomic groups[16] and ethnic groups.[17] If bullying is about power rather than an individual disorder, it should be more frequent in contexts where there is little cohesion and less equality in terms of access to resources. Indeed, bullying prevalence increases with inequality in nations,[18] classrooms,[19] and even at home.[20] Furthermore, it has been shown that interventions to reduce bullying have little success if the bully is highly popular, i.e., has social power and there is no incentive to discontinue socially enhancing behavior.[21] In contrast, victims have been described as withdrawn, unassertive, easily emotionally upset, and as having poor emotional or social understanding;[15,22] whereas bully/victims tend to be aggressive, easily angered, low on popularity, and frequently bullied by their siblings,[23] i.e., most like conduct-disordered children.

Adverse Consequences of Being Bullied

Until fairly recently, most studies on the effects of bullying were cross-sectional or just included brief follow-up periods. Thus, pre-existing mental health problems may explain that the children were bullied, rather than bullying being the "cause" of the problems. Furthermore, most studies just investigated victimization rather than also bullying perpetration and few distinguished between victims and bully/victims. However, recent longitudinal studies into adolescence,[24,25,26] early adulthood[8,9,27,28] and even into late adulthood[29] indicate that being the victim of bullying is associated with often severe mental health problems, including anxiety disorders, depression, self-harm and suicide, personality disorder,[30] and psychotic symptoms that are long lasting and persist up to 40 years later! The use of genetically sensitive designs where mono-zygotic twins (genetically identical living in the same households) but discordant for experiences of bullying were compared, showed that internalizing problems increased over time only in those who were bullied.[31] Furthermore, longitudinal studies allow for the control of pre-existing mental illness, family factors from parenting, domestic violence to abuse, and social disadvantage.[32] Thus, there is mounting evidence that being exposed to bullying as victim or bully/victim has unique adverse impact on mental health.[33] Furthermore, most recent evidence indicates that being bullied leads to highly increased difficulties in economic behavior, losing or leaving jobs, and lower income and overall poorer quality of life[29,32,34] (see Figure A-2).

The carefully controlled longitudinal studies paint a converging picture of the long-term effects of being bullied in childhood. Firstly, the effects of being bullied are found beyond other childhood adversity and adult abuse.[9] In fact, when compared to the experience of having been placed into care in childhood, the effects of frequent bullying were as detrimental 40 years later![29] Secondly, there is a dose–effect relationship between being victimized by peers and outcomes in adolescence and adulthood. Those who were bullied more frequently,[29] more severely (i.e., direct and indirectly bullied[25]) or more chronically bullied (i.e., over a longer period of time[8]) show more adverse outcome. Thirdly, even those who have escaped from

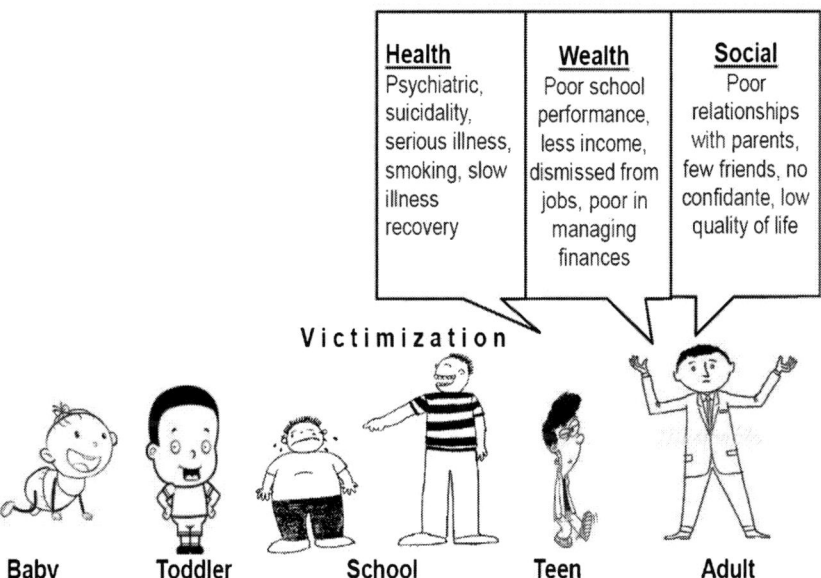

FIGURE A-2 The impact of being bullied on functioning in adulthood.[8,9,27,29,32]
SOURCE: Figure developed by Dieter Wolke.

being previously bullied at school age still show an increased risk for their health, self-worth, and quality of life years later.[24] Fourthly, where victims and bully/victims have been considered separately, bully/victims seem to show the poorest outcome ranging from mental health, to economic adaptation, social relationships to early parenthood.[9,27,32,35] Fifthly, studies that did distinguish between bullies and bully/victims found no adverse effects of being a pure bully on adverse adult outcomes. This is consistent with a view that bullies are highly sophisticated social manipulators who show little empathy and are callous.[36]

Processes

There are a variety of potential routes by which being victimized may affect later life outcomes. Being bullied may alter physiological responses to stress,[37] interact with a genetic vulnerability such as variation in the serotonin transporter (5-HTT) gene,[38] or affect telomere length (aging) or the epigenome.[39] Altered HPA-axis activity and altered cortisol responses may not only increase the risk for developing mental health problems[40] but also increase susceptibility to illness by interfering with immune responses.[41]

A recent study found that bullied children may experience higher than normal chronic inflammation and associated health problems that can persist into adulthood.[42] Blood tests for C-reactive protein (CRP), a marker of low-grade systemic inflammation in the body often associated with cardiovascular disease, metabolic syndrome, and psychological disorders, revealed that CRP levels in the blood of bullied children increased with the number of times they were bullied. Additional blood tests carried out on the children after they had reached 19 and 21 years old revealed that those who were bullied as children had CRP levels more than twice as high as bullies, whereas bullies had CRP levels lower than those who were neither bullies nor victims (see Figure A-3). Thus, bullying others appears to have a protective effect in reducing the general rise in chronic inflammation from childhood to early adulthood. This is consistent with studies showing lower inflammation for individuals with higher socioeconomic status[43] and studies with non-human primates showing health benefits for those higher in the social hierarchy.[44] The clear implication of these findings is that both ends of the continuum of social status in peer relationships are important for inflammation levels and health status.

Furthermore, experiences of threat by peers may alter cognitive responses to threatening situations[45] or affect school performance. Both altered stress responses and altered social cognition (e.g., being hypervigilant to hostile cues[46]) and neuro-circuitry[47] related to bullying exposure may affect social relationships with parents, friends, and co-workers. Finally, victimization, in particular of bully-victims, has been found to be associated

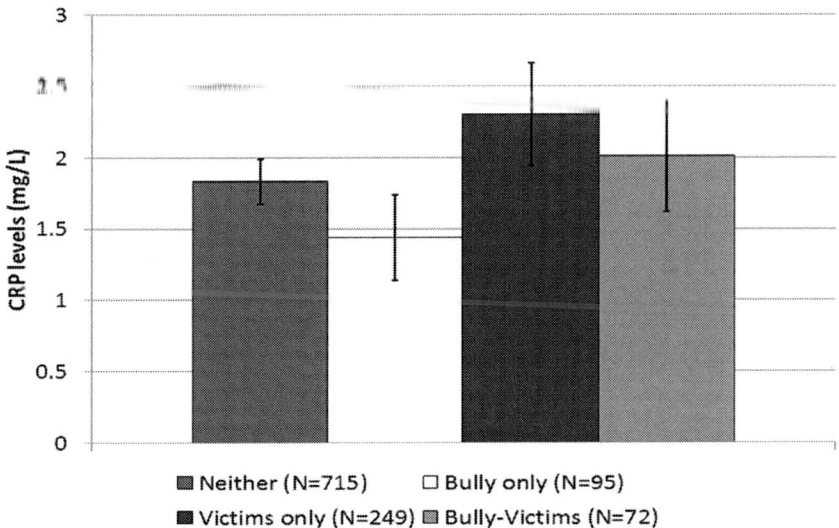

FIGURE A-3 Adjusted mean young adult CRP levels (mg/L) based on childhood/adolescent bullying status.
NOTE: These values are adjusted for baseline CRP levels as well as other CRP-related covariates. All analyses used robust standard errors to account for repeated observations.
SOURCE: Reprinted with permission from Copeland et al., 2014.

with poor concurrent academic achievement.[48] In the UK alone, more than 16,000 young people aged 11–15 are estimated to be absent from state school with bullying as the main reason, and 78,000 are absent where bullying is one of the reasons given for absence.[49] The risk of failure to complete high school or college in chronic victims or bully/victims increases the risk of poorer income and job performance.[32]

Summary and Implications

Childhood bullying has serious effects on health, leading to substantial costs for individuals, their families and society at large. In the United States, it has been estimated that preventing high school bullying results in lifetime cost benefits of more than $1.4 million per individual.[50] Many bullied children suffer in silence, and are reluctant to tell their parents or teachers about their experiences, for fear of reprisals or shame.[51] Up to 50 percent of children say they would rarely, or never, tell their parents, while between 35 percent and 60 percent would not tell their teacher.[52]

Considering this evidence of ill effects of being bullied and the fact that children will have spent much more time with their peers than their parents by the time they reach 18 years of age, it is more than surprising that childhood bullying is not at the forefront as a major public health concern.[53] Children are hardly ever asked about their peer relationships by health professionals. This is because health professionals are poorly educated about bullying and find it difficult to raise the subject or deal with it.[54] To prevent violence against oneself (e.g., self-harm) and reduce mental health problems, it is imperative to address bullying!

Key Messages

- Childhood bullying is a significant risk factor leading to harmful physical, psychological, and social effects that can last a lifetime.
- It affects children from all socioeconomic backgrounds and ethnic groups and requires universal intervention.
- There is a need for greater awareness and responsiveness in primary and secondary health care as part of a communitywide, integrated approach to stemming the effects of childhood bullying.
- Evidence-based guidance needs to be developed on how best to identify affected children in health care, provide support to children and their parents, and, where necessary, make referrals to appropriate agencies for associated physical and mental health problems.
- Effective interventions that can be delivered in primary care to minimize the consequences of being bullied are needed. These may include innovative online interventions.[55]
- New approaches are needed to channel the considerable leadership abilities and need for social recognition of bullies into socially acceptable and prosocial activities.

References

1. Olweus D. *Bullying at school: What we know and what we can do*. Wiley-Blackwell; 1993.
2. Bjorkqvist K, Lagerspetz KM, Kaukiainen A. Do girls manipulate and boys fight? Developmental trends in regard to direct and indirect aggression. *Aggressive Behavior.* 1992;18(2):117-127.
3. Wolke D, Woods S, Bloomfield L, Karstadt L. The association between direct and relational bullying and behaviour problems among primary school children. *Journal of Child Psychology and Psychiatry.* 2000;41(8):989-1002.
4. Crick NR, Grotpeter JK. Children's treatment by peers: Victims of relational and overt aggression. *Development and Psychopathology.* 1996;8(02):367-380.
5. Haynie DL, Nansel T, Eitel P, et al. Bullies, victims, and bully/victims: Distinct groups of at-risk youth. *The Journal of Early Adolescence.* 2001;21(1):29-49.

6. Boulton MJ, Smith PK. Bully/victim problems in middle-school children: Stability, self-perceived competence, peer perceptions and peer acceptance. *British Journal of Developmental Psychology.* 1994;12(3):315-329.
7. Analitis F, Velderman M, Ravens-Sieberer U. Being bullied: Associated factors in children and adolescents 8 to 18 years old in 11 European countries. *Pediatrics.* 2009;123(2):569-577.
8. Wolke D, Lereya ST, Fisher HL, Lewis G, Zammit S. Bullying in elementary school and psychotic experiences at 18 years: A longitudinal, population-based cohort study. *Psychological Medicine.* 2013;FirstView:1-13.
9. Copeland WE, Wolke D, Angold A, Costello E. Adult psychiatric outcomes of bullying and being bullied by peers in childhood and adolescence. *JAMA Psychiatry.* 2013;70(4):419-426.
10. Olweus D. Cyberbullying: An overrated phenomenon? *European Journal of Developmental Psychology.* 2012/09/01 2012;9(5):520-538.
11. Radford L, Corral S, Bradley C, Fisher H. The prevalence and impact of child maltreatment and other types of victimization in the UK: Findings from a population survey of caregivers, children and young people and young adults. *Child Abuse and Neglect.* 2013.
12. Volk AA, Camilleri JA, Dane AV, Marini ZA. Is Adolescent Bullying an Evolutionary Adaptation? *Aggressive Behavior.* 2012;38:222-238.
13. Olthof T, Goossens FA, Vermande MM, Aleva EA, van der Meulen M. Bullying as strategic behavior: Relations with desired and acquired dominance in the peer group. *Journal of School Psychology.* 2011;49(3):339-359.
14. Hawley PH, Little TD, Card NA. The myth of the alpha male: A new look at dominance-related beliefs and behaviors among adolescent males and females. *International Journal of Behavioral Development.* January 1, 2008 2008;32(1):76-88.
15. Woods S, Wolke D, Novicki S, Hall L. Emotion recognition abilities and empathy of victims of bullying. *Child Abuse and Neglect.* 2009;33(5):307-311.
16. Tippett N, Wolke D. Socioeconomic Status and Bullying: A Meta-Analysis. *American Journal of Public Health.* 2014:e1-e12.
17. Tippett N, Wolke D, Platt L. Ethnicity and bullying involvement in a national UK youth sample. *Journal of Adolescence.* 2013;36(4):639-649.
18. Elgar FJ, Craig W, Boyce W, Morgan A, Vella-Zarb R. Income Inequality and School Bullying: Multilevel Study of Adolescents in 37 Countries. *The Journal of Adolescent Health: Official publication of the Society for Adolescent Medicine.* 10/01 2009;45(4):351-359.
19. Garandeau C, Lee I, Salmivalli C. Inequality Matters: Classroom Status Hierarchy and Adolescents' Bullying. *Journal of Youth and Adolescence.* 2013/10/16 2013:1-11.
20. Wolke D, Skew AJ. Bullying among siblings. *International Journal of Adolescent Medicine and Health.* 2012;24(1):17-25.
21. Garandeau CF, Lee IA, Salmivalli C. Differential effects of the KiVa anti-bullying program on popular and unpopular bullies. *Journal of Applied Developmental Psychology.* 2014;35(1):44-50.
22. Camodeca M, Goossens FA, Schuengel C, Terwogt MM. Links between social informative processing in middle childhood and involvement in bullying. *Aggressive Behavior.* 2003;29(2):116-127.
23. Wolke D, Skew A. Family factors, bullying victimisation and well-being in adolescents. *Longitudinal and Life Course Studies.* 2012;3(1):101-119.
24. Bogart LM, Elliott MN, Klein DJ, et al. Peer victimization in fifth grade and health in tenth grade. *Pediatrics.* February 17, 2014.
25. Zwierzynska K, Wolke D, Lereya TS. Peer victimization in childhood and internalizing problems in adolescence: a prospective longitudinal study. *Journal of Abnormal Child Psychology.* 2013/02/01 2013;41(2):309-323.

26. Lereya ST, Winsper C, Heron J, et al. Being bullied during childhood and the prospective pathways to self-harm in late adolescence. *Journal of the American Academy of Child and Adolescent Psychiatry.* 2013;52(6):608-618.e602.
27. Sourander A, Jensen P, Ronning JA, et al. What is the early adulthood outcome of boys who bully or are bullied in childhood? The Finnish "From a Boy to a Man" study. *Pediatrics.* August 1, 2007;120(2):397-404.
28. Klomek AB, Sourander A, Niemelä S, et al. Childhood bullying behaviors as a risk for suicide attempts and completed suicides: A population-based birth cohort study. *Journal of the American Academy of Child and Adolescent Psychiatry.* 2009;48(3):254-261.
29. Takizawa R, Maughan B, Arseneault L. Adult Health outcomes of childhood bullying victimization: Evidence from a five-decade longitudinal british birth cohort. *American Journal of Psychiatry.* 2014:online first.
30. Wolke D, Schreier A, Zanarini MC, Winsper C. Bullied by peers in childhood and borderline personality symptoms at 11 years of age: A prospective study. *Journal of Child Psychology and Psychiatry.* 2012;53(8):846-855.
31. Arseneault L, Milne BJ, Taylor A, et al. Being bullied as an environmentally mediated contributing factor to children's internalizing problems: A study of twins discordant for victimization. *Arch Pediatr Adolesc Med.* February 1, 2008 2008;162(2):145-150.
32. Wolke D, Copeland WE, Angold A, Costello EJ. Impact of bullying in childhood on adult health, wealth, crime, and social outcomes. *Psychological Science.* August 19, 2013 2013;24(10):1958-1970.
33. Arseneault L, Bowes L, Shakoor S. Bullying victimization in youths and mental health problems: "Much ado about nothing"? *Psychological Medicine.* 2010;40(5):717-729.
34. Brown S, Taylor K. Bullying, education and earnings: Evidence from the National Child Development Study. *Economics of Education Review.* 2008;27(4):387-401.
35. Lehti V, Klomek AB, Tamminen T, et al. Childhood bullying and becoming a young father in a national cohort of Finnish boys. *Scandinavian Journal of Psychology.* 2012;53(6):461-466.
36. Sutton J, Smith PK, Swettenham J. Social cognition and bullying: Social inadequacy or skilled manipulation? *British Journal of Developmental Psychology.* 1999;17:435-450.
37. Ouellet-Morin I, Danese A, Bowes L, et al. A discordant monozygotic twin design shows blunted cortisol reactivity among bullied children. *Journal of the American Academy of Child and Adolescent Psychiatry.* 2011;50(6):574-582.e573.
38. Sugden K, Arseneault L, Harrington H, Moffitt TE, Williams B, Caspi A. Serotonin transporter gene moderates the development of emotional problems among children following bullying victimization. *Journal of the American Academy of Child and Adolescent Psychiatry.* 2010;49(8):830-840.
39. Shalev I, Moffitt TE, Sugden K, et al. Exposure to violence during childhood is associated with telomere erosion from 5 to 10 years of age: A longitudinal study. *Mol Psychiatry.* 2012;18:576-581.
40. Harkness KL, Stewart JG, Wynne-Edwards KE. Cortisol reactivity to social stress in adolescents: Role of depression severity and child maltreatment. *Psychoneuroendocrino.* 2011;36(2):173-181.
41. Segerstrom SC, Miller GE. Psychological Stress and the human immune system: A meta-analytic study of 30 years of inquiry. *Psychological Bulletin.* 2004;30(4):601-630.
42. Copeland WE, Wolke D, Lereya ST, Shanahan L, Worthman C, Costello EJ. Childhood bullying involvement predicts low-grade systemic inflammation into adulthood. 2014. *PNAS: Proceedings of the National Academy of Sciences of the United States of America* 111(21):7570-7575.

43. Jousilahti P, Salomaa V, Rasi V, Vahtera E, Palosuo T. Association of markers of systemic inflammation, C-reactive protein, serum amyloid A, and fibrinogen, with socioeconomic status. *Journal of Epidemiology and Community Health.* September 1, 2003 2003;57(9):730-733.
44. Sapolsky RM. The influence of social hierarchy on primate health. *Science.* April 29, 2005 2005;308(5722):648-652.
45. Mezulis AH, Abramson LY, Hyde JS, Hankin BL. Is there a universal positivity bias in attributions? A meta-analytic review of individual, developmental, and cultural differences in the self-serving attributional bias. *Psychological Bulletin.* 2004;130(5):711-747.
46. van Dam DS, van der Ven E, Velthorst E, Selten JP, Morgan C, de Haan L. Childhood bullying and the association with psychosis in non-clinical and clinical samples: A review and meta-analysis. *Psychological Medicine.* 2012;42(12):2463-2474
47. Teicher MH, Samson JA, Sheu YS, Polcari A, McGreenery CE. Hurtful words: Association of exposure to peer verbal abuse with elevated psychiatric symptom scores and corpus callosum abnormalities. *Am J Psychiat.* 2010;167(12):1464-1471.
48. Nakamoto J, Schwartz D. Is peer victimization associated with academic achievement? A meta-analytic review. *Social Development.* 2010;19(2):221-242.
49. Brown V, Clery E, Ferguson C. Estimating the prevalence of young people absent from school due to bullying. *National Centre for Social Research.* 2011;1:1-61.
50. Masiello M, Schroeder D, Barto S, et al. 2012. *The cost benefit: A first-time analysis of savings.* Highmark Foundation.
51. Chamberlain T, George N, Golden S, Walker F, Benton T. 2010. *Tellus4 national report*: National Foundation for Educational Research. The Department for Children, Schools, and Families.
52. Radford L, Corral S, Bradley C, Fisher HL. 2013. The prevalence and impact of child maltreatment and other types of victimization in the UK: Findings from a population survey of caregivers, children and young people and young adults. *Child Abuse and Neglect.* 37(10):801-813.
53. Scrabstein JC, Merrick J. 2012. Bullying is everywhere: An expanding scope of public health concerns. *International Journal of Adolescent Medicine and Health.* 24(1):1.
54. Dale J, Russell R, Wolke D. 2014. Intervening in primary care against childhood bullying: An increasingly pressing public health need. *Journal of the Royal Society of Medicine.* 107(6):219-223.
55. Sapouna M, Wolke D, Vannini N, et al. 2010. Virtual learning intervention to reduce bullying victimization in primary school: A controlled trial. *Journal of Child Psychology and Psychiatry.* 51(1):104-112.

Appendix B

Workshop Agenda

Mental Health and Violence:
Opportunities for Prevention and Early Intervention
A Workshop of the
National Academies of Sciences, Engineering, and Medicine's
Forum on Global Violence Prevention
February 26–27, 2014

Keck Center of the National Academies of
Sciences, Engineering, and Medicine
500 Fifth Street NW, Washington, DC 20001
Rooms 100 and 101
(Room 101 is the overflow room with webcasting)

The goal of this workshop is to examine the evidence, research, and perspectives about mental health and violence to facilitate enhanced global action and policies for the prevention of violence associated with mental illness, as well as treat its consequences that occur around the world.

The workshop will explore a continuum of approaches for improving both mental health and violence prevention with the following objectives:

- To arrive at a better understanding of the intersection of mental health and violence, including the following:
    o The relationship between mental health and risk of both violence perpetration and victimization, as well as the mental health consequences of exposure to violence
    o The extent to which improved mental health functioning and mental health services can address current concerns about violence in society
- To explore a new model of the intersection of mental health and violence that will be useful for improving outcomes. The model will include the following:
    o A description of mental health function as a continuum from optimal to dysfunctional, with problems ranging from minor to serious distress to antisocial behavior to severe mental illness
    o Perpetration of violence, victims of violence, and exposure to violence
    o Interpersonal, self-directed, and collective violence
    o Neurobiology of violent behavior
    o Multiple ecological levels to be considered
    o A life-course/developmental perspective
    o Means of violence perpetration, including access to weapons
    o Identification of the multiple sectors that must be involved, as well as their intersection

Day 1: Wednesday, February 26, 2014

8:00 AM   Continental Breakfast

8:10 AM   Welcome from the National Academies of Sciences, Engineering, and Medicine

- PATRICK KELLEY, *National Academies of Sciences, Engineering, and Medicine's Board on Global Health and African Science Academy Development Initiative*

8:15 AM   Welcome and Workshop Goals

- PEGGY MURRAY, *National Institute on Alcohol Abuse and Alcoholism, Workshop Planning Committee Co-Chair*
- MARK ROSENBERG, *The Task Force for Global Health, Workshop Planning Committee Co-Chair*

8:45 AM   Opening Keynote

The intersection of mental health and violence is a critical and complex public health problem. Considering the importance and complexity of the issue, this keynote address will focus on: What do we know? What do we need to know? And, what can we do now to improve outcomes in this area?

- THOMAS INSEL, *National Institute of Mental Health*

Part I: Understanding the Problem
9:15 AM–2:00 PM

The objectives of this session include highlighting the intersection of mental health and violence through a common understanding of terms, a description of the risk and protective factors that come into play on various ecological levels, and identification of the significant neurocognitive mechanisms related to violence. Additionally, a panel of individuals will share their lived experiences and perspectives of mental health and violence.

9:15 AM   Operational Definitions for the Workshop
This presentation will provide operational definitions of key terms for the new model being explored during the workshop, including mental health, mental illness, violence, conduct disorder, alcohol and substance use disorders, perpetrators, and victims.

- VICKIE MAYS, *University of California, Los Angeles*

9:45 AM   Ecological Framework
This session will present an overview and discussions of risk and protective factors and intervention points related to mental health and violence at the individual, relationship, community, and societal levels.

- ERIC CAINE, *University of Rochester Medical Center*
- JANIS JENKINS, *University of California, San Diego*

10:30 AM   BREAK

10:45 AM   What Is the Relationship Between Various Mental Illnesses and Violence?
This presentation will include what is known about the relationship between various mental illnesses and violence and why it is important for what is known to be represented accurately. The presentation will be followed by discussion with the workshop participants.

- MARK ROSENBERG

11:30 AM   Understanding the Neurocognitive Mechanisms of Violent Behavior
This presentation will include a sketch of some of the neurocognitive mechanisms related to violence and how such mechanisms are affected by various factors, including stress and alcohol, and how they can be used for prediction. The presentation will be followed by discussion with the workshop participants.

- JAMES BLAIR, *National Institute of Mental Health*

12:00 PM   LUNCH

1:00 PM   Experiences and Perspectives Related to Mental Health and Violence
This session includes experiences and perspectives of mental health and violence, including stigma, victimization, and vulnerability, as well as media depictions of the relationship between mental illness and violence. The presentations will be followed by discussion with the workshop participants.

Moderator/Panelist: Daniel Fisher, *Riverside Community Mental Health Center*
- Elyn Saks, *University of Southern California* (by videoconference)
- Harvey Rosenthal, *New York Association of Psychiatric Rehabilitation Services, Inc.*

Discussant: Robert Bernstein, *Judge David L. Bazelon Center for Mental Health Law*

Part II: Exploring a New Model of the Intersection of Mental Health and Violence
Day 1: 2:00–5:15 PM and Day 2: 8:20 AM–2:15 PM

The objectives for this session are to explore a multifactorial model of the intersection of mental health and violence and to illuminate the current evidence of the effectiveness of key interventions for preventing violence and promoting mental health. Topics to be covered include detecting and assessing risk for mental health dysfunction and violence; the values and limitations of current assessments; the role of varying means of violence; the relationship of alcohol and alcohol use disorders in occurrences of violence; the opportunities in mental health service delivery for preventing violence and providing care to victims, perpetrators, and observers; and the critical significance of the interface between the criminal justice community and individuals with mental illness in preventing violence victimization and perpetration.

2:00 PM   Detecting and Assessing Mental Health Dysfunction and Risk for Violence
This panel will explore current capabilities to identify and assess mental health dysfunction and the risk for violence and how this affects treatment. Panelists will discuss both the

values and limitations of the current state of risk assessment and how assessment can be improved. The presentations will be followed by discussion with the workshop participants.

Moderator: VICKIE MAYS
- SEENA FAZEL, *University of Oxford, United Kingdom*
- DUSTIN PARDINI, *University of Pittsburgh*
- DIETER WOLKE, *University of Warwick, United Kingdom*

3:30 PM **BREAK**

3:45 PM **Mental Health and Means of Violence**
The means of violence vary by nation, culture, and often by circumstances of convenience. This panel will explore issues of access to means that include the legal and constitutional rights of individuals and the public at large. Panelists will examine practices and tools that show promise in the prevention of violence while balancing the needs and rights for individual and information privacy. The panel will also discuss the need for improvements in early and correct identification of people who are at risk for committing violence that do not create or compound barriers to seek needed care. Lastly, the panel will discuss what is needed to improve research and intervention design to contribute to better outcomes in violence prevention and early intervention. Panelists will present on firearms, homicide, and nonfatal injuries and pesticides, other means, and suicide. The presentations will be followed by discussion with the workshop participants.

Moderator: MARK ROSENBERG
- DANIEL WEBSTER, *Johns Hopkins Bloomberg School of Public Health*
- MICHAEL PHILLIPS, *Shanghai Jiao Tong University School of Medicine*

Discussant: MIKE LUO, The New York Times *(by telephone)*

5:15 PM **Summary of Day 1 and Wrap Up**

- PEGGY MURRAY

5:30 PM **Adjourn Day 1**

Day 2: Thursday, February 27, 2014

8:00 AM   Continental Breakfast

8:15 AM   Opening and Summary of Day 1

- PEGGY MURRAY
- MARK ROSENBERG

8:20 AM   Alcohol, Alcohol Use Disorders, and Violence

Alcohol is one of the most significant risk factors for violence. At the same time, alcohol addiction and the harmful use of alcohol are among the identified alcohol use disorders in the *Diagnostic and Statistical Manual of Mental Disorders, Fifth Edition*. This panel will focus on the unique role of alcohol consumption and alcohol use disorders in the occurrence of violence and current developments in interventions to address it. Presentations will cover a range of scientific and policy-focused activities ranging from basic research to human laboratory studies of behavior, and finally, evidence-based interventions and effective alcohol control policies. The presentations will be followed by discussion with the workshop participants.

Moderator: PEGGY MURRAY
- KLAUS MICZEK, *Tufts University*
- KENNETH LEONARD, *University at Buffalo*
- TOBEN NELSON, *University of Minnesota*
- RONALDO LARANJEIRA, *Universidade Federal de São Paulo, Brazil*

9:45 AM   Violence Prevention and Mental Health Services

This panel will describe how mental health services present the opportunity to prevent violence while providing care to those in need including victims and perpetrators of violence. Panelists will explore service and care access, current capabilities for risk identification and risk reduction, opportunities for early intervention and response, and strategies for improvement of mental health services for prevention and early intervention. The presentations will be followed by discussion with the workshop participants.

Moderator: A.J. ALLEN, *Eli Lilly and Company*
- COLLEEN BARRY, *Johns Hopkins Bloomberg School of Public Health*
- SHARON STEPHAN, *University of Maryland*
- DÉVORA KESTEL, *Pan American Health Organization*

11:00 AM BREAK

11:15 AM Interface with the Justice Community and Opportunities for Intervention

In the United States in the 1960s, deinstitutionalization of persons with mental illness shifted psychiatric care from long-term inpatient hospitals to community mental health and other outpatient facilities. Unintended consequences, including lack of adequate funding to mental health centers, lack of employment opportunities, and a dearth of low-income housing resulted in many people not receiving either adequate treatment or housing. Many mentally ill people were on the streets and had significant interface with the criminal justice system. This panel will examine that interface across the three components of criminal justice: law enforcement, criminal courts, and incarcerations. With a focus on each of the components and with a global perspective, panelists will present the challenges to balancing civil rights and public interest, the opportunities for creative interventions, and the obstacles and risks that remain. The presentations will be followed by discussion with the workshop participants.

Moderator: MADELON BARANOSKI, *Yale University*
- SHELDON GREENBERG, *Johns Hopkins University School of Education*
- RAY KOTWICKI, *Skyland Trail*
- DAVID WEXLER, *International Network of Therapeutic Jurisprudence*
- PATRICK FOX, *University of Colorado*

12:45 PM LUNCH

1:45 PM How Are Interventions Being Evaluated? How Can Evaluation Be Improved?

The principal goals of prevention science are to improve public health by identifying alterable risk and protective factors and to assess the effectiveness of prevention interventions including optimal modes for diffusion and dissemination. Theories of human development and social ecology are often used to design interventions that aim to elicit behavior change, especially those that examine violence or mental health from a life-course perspective. This session will examine the successful use and limitations of randomized controlled trials for determining efficacy of interventions for violence prevention; the alternative rigorous evaluation designs to evaluate their effectiveness and impact; and how well the programs are being implemented. Evaluation findings can lead to program or intervention adaptation, quality improvement for existing programs, improved design for future interventions, and sustainability for effective interventions. Partners to engage in evaluations and program impact improvement efforts will also be discussed.

- HENDRICKS BROWN, *Northwestern University*

Moderator for question-and-answer session only:

- KIMBERLY SCOTT, *Health and Medicine Division*

**Part III: The Way Forward
2:15–4:00 PM**

The objective for this session is to examine how to improve outcomes with respect to mental health and violence. The focus will be on three areas: research, policy change, and program development. Questions to be addressed include the following: How do we reframe the issue in a manner that will promote understanding and improve both mental health promotion and violence prevention? What are the most important research questions that need to be addressed? How do we communicate more effectively with the various constituencies that need to be involved? How do we mobilize the various sectors and actors who have important roles in research, program and policy development, financing, and implementation? What are the significant barriers and how can they be overcome? How should we move forward? What are the priority items for the agenda going forward? Panelists have been drawn from the perspectives of mental health services, criminal justice, culture and anthropology, mental health services in low- and middle-income countries, and violence prevention.

2:15 PM   Reflections from the Workshop and the Way Forward

Moderator: MARK ROSENBERG
- COLLEEN BARRY, *Johns Hopkins Bloomberg School of Public Health*
- SHELDON GREENBERG, *Johns Hopkins University School of Education*
- JANIS JENKINS, *University of California, San Diego*
- DÉVORA KESTEL, *Pan American Health Organization*
- JAMES MERCY, *Centers for Disease Control and Prevention*

3:30 PM   Open Discussion

4:00 PM   Workshop Adjournment

Appendix C

Workshop Speaker Biographies

As of February 2014

Albert J. Allen, M.D., Ph.D., is the senior medical fellow with responsibility for bioethics and pediatric capabilities at Lilly Research Labs, Eli Lilly and Company, Indianapolis, Indiana. Dr. Allen received a B.S. in chemistry and an M.S. in biochemistry from The University of Chicago and an M.D. and a Ph.D. from the University of Iowa. In 1995, Dr. Allen and his mentors, Dr. Susan Swedo and Dr. Henrietta Leonard, shared the American Academy of Child and Adolescent Psychiatry's Norbert and Charlotte Rieger Award for Scientific Achievement for their research on possible infection-triggered cases of obsessive compulsive disorder (OCD) and tics. In the same year, he joined the Institute for Juvenile Research at the University of Illinois at Chicago, where he was an assistant professor in child and adolescent psychiatry. In Chicago, he established and ran a pediatric OCD and tic disorders clinic. He joined Eli Lilly in April 2000 and, in late 2003, he became global medical director of the Strattera Product Team. In October 2004, he was made global medical director of the Neuroscience Platform Team. In the past few years, he was the senior medical director globally for attention deficit hyperactivity disorder (ADHD) and related disorders. He was also extensively involved with several activities related to pediatric studies and global regulatory activities across Lilly's neuroscience products, and has participated in pharmaceutical industry activities in pediatric drug development and the assessment of drugs in development for human abuse liability. He chairs Lilly's Bioethics Advisory Committee and co-chairs Lilly's Pediatric Steering Committee, and he is the past chair of Lilly's Drug Abuse Liability and Dependence Advisory Committee. Dr. Allen is a member of the American Psychiatric Association and the American Academy of Child and Adolescent Psychiatry. He is also a specialty fellow of the American Academy of Pediatrics. In July 2012, he was appointed to the Secretary's Advisory Committee on Human Research Protections, a federal advisory committee in the U.S. Department of Health and Human Services (HHS) that provides expert advice and recommendations to the Secretary of HHS on issues and topics pertaining to the protection of human research subjects.

Paul S. Appelbaum, M.D., is the Elizabeth K. Dollard Professor of Psychiatry, Medicine, and Law, and director of the Division of Psychiatry, Law, and Ethics, Department of Psychiatry, College of Physicians and Surgeons of Columbia University; a research psychiatrist at the New York State Psychiatric Institute; and an affiliated faculty member, Columbia Law School. He directs Columbia's Center for Research on Ethical, Legal, & Social Implications of Psychiatric, Neurologic, & Behavioral Genetics, and heads the Clinical Research Ethics Core for Columbia's Clinical and Translational Science Award program. His research interests include the prediction and management of violent behavior by people with mental illness. He is the author of many articles and books on law and ethics in clinical practice and research. Dr. Appelbaum is a graduate of Columbia College, received his M.D. from Harvard Medical School, and completed his residency in psychiatry at the Massachusetts Mental Health Center of the Harvard Medical School in Boston. He is past president of the American Psychiatric Association and a member of the National Academy of Medicine.

Madelon Baranoski, Ph.D., M.S.N., is an associate professor in the Department of Psychiatry, Law and Psychiatry Division, of Yale University School of Medicine, and faculty in the Immigration and Veterans Clinics in the Yale Law School. She is also vice chair of the Yale University Human Investigation Committees and the director of the New Haven Jail Diversion Program of the Connecticut Department of Mental Health and Addiction Services and the Connecticut Mental Health Center. Her research interests include violence risk assessment and management, cultural manifestations of trauma and depression, assessment of competency in court-ordered evaluations, and state-of-mind evaluations. Dr. Baranoski received her B.S.N. from the University of Maryland Walter Reed Army Institute in 1969, her M.S.N. from Yale University School of Nursing in 1974, and her Ph.D. in clinical and developmental psychology from the University of Pennsylvania in 1982. She has published and presented on risk assessment and management in psychiatric populations.

Colleen L. Barry, Ph.D., M.P.P., is an associate professor and an associate chair for research and practice in the Department of Health Policy and

Management at the Johns Hopkins Bloomberg School of Public Health. Professor Barry conducts policy analysis and political communication research with a focus on vulnerable populations and often stigmatized health conditions, including mental illness, substance use, and obesity. Much of her current research involves examining the implications of various aspects of the Patient Protection and Affordable Care Act on persons with mental illness and/or substance use disorders. She has also led studies examining public opinion and political persuasion in the context of childhood obesity, mental illness, and gun policy.

Robert Bernstein, Ph.D., is a psychologist with a strong interest in ensuring meaningful community participation and promoting the consumer voice within mental health systems, particularly for individuals who are marginalized or neglected by public systems. For 19 years before his appointment to this post, Dr. Bernstein was the architect and director of one of the nation's oldest and largest mental health and aging programs. NSO-Older Adult Services in Detroit, Michigan, featured an innovative system that blended in-home services and advocacy to support older adults with persistent mental illnesses in integrated community settings. In addition to his work with that trailblazing program, he ran a private practice where he specialized in treating children and adolescents. Dr. Bernstein is a leader in the field of mental health policy and advocacy. He has published several important papers and served as an expert in litigation concerning such areas as conditions in psychiatric institutions, the use of seclusion and restraint, community mental health, older adult needs, and fair housing. He also contributed to the preparation of the 1999 Surgeon General's Report on Mental Health and the President's New Freedom Commission on Mental Health.

James Blair, M.D., is the chief of the Unit on Affective Cognitive Neuroscience at the National Institute of Mental Health (NIMH). Dr. Blair received a doctoral degree in psychology from University College London in 1993 under the supervision of Professor John Morton. Following graduation, he was awarded a Wellcome Trust Mental Health Research Fellowship, which he held at the Medical Research Council Cognitive Development Unit for 3 years. Subsequently, he moved to the Institute of Cognitive Neuroscience, University College London. There, with Uta Frith, he helped form and co-lead the Developmental Disorders group, and was ultimately appointed senior lecturer. He joined the NIMH Intramural Research Program in 2002. Dr. Blair's primary research interest involves understanding the neurocognitive systems mediating affect in humans and how these become dysfunctional in mood and anxiety disorders. His primary clinical focus is on understanding the dysfunction of affect-related systems in youth with specific forms of conduct disorder.

His research approach includes techniques employed in cognitive neuroscience (both neuropsychology and functional imaging), psychopharmacology, and molecular genetics.

C. Hendricks Brown, Ph.D., is a professor in the Departments of Psychiatry and Behavioral Sciences and Preventive Medicine in the Northwestern University Feinberg School of Medicine. He also holds adjunct appointments in the Departments of Biostatistics and Mental Health at the Johns Hopkins Bloomberg School of Public Health, as well as in the Department of Public Health Sciences at the Miller School of Medicine at the University of Miami. He directs the National Institute on Drug Abuse–funded Center for Prevention Implementation Methodology (Ce-PIM) for Drug Abuse and Sexual Risk Behavior and an NIMH-funded study to synthesize findings from individual-level data across multiple randomized trials for adolescent depression. Recently, his work has focused on the prevention of drug abuse, conduct disorder, depression, and particularly the prevention of suicide. Dr. Brown has been a member of the National Academies of Sciences, Engineering, and Medicine's Committee on Prevention Science, and serves on numerous federal panels, advisory boards, and editorial boards.

Eric Caine, M.D., has investigated factors that contribute to suicide, with a focus on links to unemployment, choice of specific methods, burdens of suicide, and attempts during young and middle adulthood. Past research has focused on military personnel and their families in the areas of intimate partner and family violence and suicide. Currently, his work has addressed public health approaches to prevention that complement individually oriented treatments. He has been the principal investigator of multiple National Institutes of Health (NIH) research and training grants related to suicide research and prevention. Since 2001, he has led a series of collaborative initiatives in China that deal with suicide prevention, the delivery of mental health services in developing countries, and the potential for public health approaches to reduce injuries and deaths.

Seena Fazel, M.D., F.R.C.Psych., is a Wellcome Trust senior research fellow in clinical science at the University of Oxford, and a consultant forensic psychiatrist at Oxford Health National Health Service (NHS) Foundation Trust. His research work focuses on relationship between severe mental illness and violent crime, violence risk assessment, and the mental health and the suicide risk of prisoners. He has served on advisory boards for NHS research funding committees and the crime reduction charity Nacro, and has given evidence to the U.K. Government Justice Select Committee and the United Nations–backed Khmer Rouge war crimes tribunal.

Daniel Fisher, M.D., Ph.D., obtained a Ph.D. in biochemistry to discover the possible chemical basis of mental health issues. While carrying out neurochemical research at the National Institute of Mental Health, Dr. Fisher was diagnosed with schizophrenia. He recovered through building meaningful relationships. He found a biochemical explanation of behavior too alienating; to humanize the mental health system, he obtained an M.D. at The George Washington University Medical School and completed psychiatric training at Harvard University. Dr. Fisher worked for 25 years as a community psychiatrist at a mental health center, founded the National Empowerment Center, has been a member of the New Freedom Commission on Mental Health, and helped organize the National Coalition for Mental Health Recovery. He has given more than 1,000 speeches and workshops on recovery and peer support across the United States and in 12 countries. He is on the faculty of the University of Massachusetts Department of Psychiatry, where he is helping to adapt Open Dialogue to the United States. Dr. Fisher helped peers in Louisiana respond to the emotional crises following Hurricanes Katrina and Rita. Based on his post-Katrina experiences, he helped develop Emotional CPR.

Patrick Fox, M.D., completed his residency training in general adult and forensic psychiatry at the Yale School of Medicine in 1999. He is board certified in Adult General and Forensic Psychiatry. Additionally, he currently serves on the Forensic Examination Committee for the American Board of Psychiatry and Neurology. He has presented nationally and internationally on seclusion and restraint reform, physician-assisted suicide, mental health reform, sex offender management, violence risk management, outpatient civil commitment, and jail diversion programs. He has also served on state panels addressing access to care for and management of youth with psychiatric disabilities, sex offender registration, sexually violent predator statutes, and civil commitment. Following his completion of residency and fellowship training, Dr. Fox remained on the faculty at Yale as an assistant professor, working initially as a consulting forensic psychiatrist for the Connecticut Department of Mental Health and Addiction Services, and later serving as director for the Whiting Forensic Division, Connecticut's maximum security forensic hospital. Additionally, he was deputy director for Yale's Forensic Psychiatry Training Program from 2007 to 2012. In 2012, he took a position as attending psychiatrist for the Denver County Sheriffs' Department, managing the city jail's most acutely ill inmates. In April 2013, Dr. Fox was appointed deputy director of clinical services for the Colorado Department of Human Services' Office of Behavioral Health. He has been serving as acting director for the Office of Behavioral Health since October 2013. In this capacity, he is responsible for overseeing all administrative and clinical services related to the provision of mental health and substance abuse treatment for the office.

Sheldon Greenberg, Ph.D., is a professor of management in the School of Education, Division of Public Safety Leadership at the Johns Hopkins School of Education. He served as associate dean for more than a decade, during which time he led the Police Executive Leadership Program and established university partnerships with the U.S. Secret Service and the U.S. Immigration and Customs Enforcement. For almost 2 years, Dr. Greenberg served as associate dean and interim director of the Johns Hopkins University Division of Business and Management (currently the Carey Business School). His primary research interests are police patrol, the relationship between police and public health, police organizational structure, highway safety, campus and school safety, the role of the police in community development, and community organizing. Before joining Johns Hopkins University, Dr. Greenberg served as associate director of the Police Executive Research Forum, the nation's largest law enforcement think tank and center for research. He began his career with the Howard County, Maryland, Police Department, where he served as a patrol officer, supervisor, director of the police academy, director of research and planning, and commander of the Administrative Services Bureau. He worked with the U.S. Marshals Service, U.S. Border Patrol, U.S. Department of Justice, and U.S. Department of State, as well as with police agencies in Cyprus, the Czech Republic, Hungary, Jordan, Kenya, Pakistan, and Panama. Dr. Greenberg has served on national commissions and task forces on violence in schools, race-based profiling, police response to people who have mental illness, police recruiting, highway safety, military deployment, and homeland defense. He serves also as a member of the Federal Law Enforcement Training Accreditation Board. Dr. Greenberg is the author of numerous articles and several books, including *Stress and the Helping Professions*, *Stress and the Teaching Profession*, and *On the Dotted Line*, a guide to hiring and retaining police executives. He has completed his fourth book, *Mastery of Police Patrol*, which will be published by Pearson Prentice Hall, and is working on his fifth book on managing community fear.

Thomas R. Insel, M.D., is the director of the National Institute of Mental Health (NIMH), the component of the National Institutes of Health (NIH) committed to research on mental disorders. Dr. Insel has served as director of this $1.5 billion agency since 2002. During his tenure, he has focused on the genetics and neurobiology of mental disorders, as well as transforming approaches to diagnosis and treatment. Before serving as NIMH director, Dr. Insel was professor of psychiatry at Emory University, where he was founding director of the Center for Behavioral Neuroscience and director of the Yerkes Regional Primate Center in Atlanta. Dr. Insel's research has examined the neural basis of complex social behaviors, including maternal care and attachment. A member of the National Academy of Medicine, he has received numerous national and international awards and served in several leadership roles at NIH.

Janis Jenkins, Ph.D., received her Ph.D. from the University of California, Los Angeles, and completed her postdoctoral training in clinically relevant medical anthropology at Harvard Medical School. She is internationally recognized for her expertise on cultural and mental health. Her principal interests include the course and outcome of major mental illness, psychopharmacology, ethnicity, violence, adolescence, resilience, and qualitative methods. Her research has been conducted with Latino and Latin American immigrants and refugees, along with Euro-American, African American, and Native American populations. As co-principal investigator for the National Institute of Mental Health (NIMH)-funded study "Southwest Youth and the Experience of Psychiatric Treatment," Dr. Jenkins and her team have investigated psychiatric disorders, cultural meaning, and violence among adolescents who have received inpatient treatment in New Mexico. Dr. Jenkins has been on faculty at Harvard University, Case Western Reserve University, and University of California, San Diego, where she is professor of anthropology and adjunct professor of psychiatry. She has been principal investigator for a series of NIMH-funded studies on culture and mental health. She has also been awarded funding by the School for Advanced Research and the National Alliance for Research on Schizophrenia and Depression. Dr. Jenkins has served as a member of three Scientific Review Groups at NIMH. She is a member of the Institute for Advanced Studies in Princeton, New Jersey (in residence during academic year 2011–2012). She has been visiting scholar-in-residence at the Russell Sage Foundation in New York City, the Institute of Social Medicine in Rio de Janeiro, and Distinguished Visiting Faculty at Monash University in Melbourne, Australia. She has published widely in scientific journals, including *American Journal of Psychiatry*, *British Journal of Psychiatry*, and *Medical Anthropology Quarterly*. She has published two edited volumes: *Schizophrenia, Culture, and Subjectivity: The Edge of Experience* (with R. J. Barrett) by Cambridge University Press (2004) and *Pharmaceutical Self: The Global Shaping of Experience in an Age of Psychopharmacology* (School for Advanced Research, 2011).

Patrick W. Kelley, M.D., Dr.P.H., joined the National Academies of Sciences, Engineering, and Medicine in July 2003 as the director of the Board on Global Health. He was subsequently appointed as the director of the Board on African Science Academy Development. Dr. Kelley has overseen a portfolio of National Academies expert consensus studies and convening activities on subjects as wide ranging as the evaluation of the President's Emergency Plan for AIDS Relief (PEPFAR); the U.S. commitment to global health; sustainable surveillance for zoonotic infections; substandard, falsified, and counterfeit drugs; innovations in health professional education; cardiovascular disease prevention in low- and middle-income countries; interpersonal violence prevention in low- and middle-income countries; and microbial threats to health. He also directs a unique capacity-building effort, the African Science Academy Development Initiative, which over 11 years aims to strengthen the capacity of eight African academies to provide independent, evidence-based advice to their governments on scientific matters.

Before joining the National Academies, Dr. Kelley served in the U.S. Army for more than 23 years as a physician, residency director, epidemiologist, and program manager. In his last U.S. Department of Defense (DoD) position, Dr. Kelley founded and directed the DoD Global Emerging Infections Surveillance and Response System. This responsibility entailed managing surveillance and capacity-building partnerships with numerous elements of the federal government and with health ministries in more than 45 developing countries. He also founded the DoD Accession Medical Standards Analysis and Research Activity and served as the specialty editor for a landmark two-volume textbook, titled *Military Preventive Medicine: Mobilization and Deployment*. Dr. Kelley is an experienced communicator having lectured in English or Spanish in over 20 countries. He has authored or co-authored more than 70 scholarly papers, book chapters, and monographs and has supervised the completion of more than 25 National Academies consensus reports and workshop summaries. While at the National Academies, he has obtained grants and contracts for work conducted by his unit from more than 60 governmental and nongovernmental sources. Dr. Kelley obtained his M.D. from the University of Virginia and his Dr.P.H. in epidemiology from the Johns Hopkins Bloomberg School of Public Health. He has also been awarded two honorary doctoral degrees and is board certified in Preventive Medicine and Public Health.

Dévora Kestel, M.Sc., M.P.H., is a mental health regional adviser at the Pan American Health Organization (PAHO). She is Argentinean and obtained her M.Sc. in psychology (Universidad Nacional de La Plata). She later earned an M.Sc. in public health at the London School of Hygiene and Tropical Medicine. After completing her university studies in Argentina, she moved to Italy, where she worked for 10 years in the development and supervision of community-based mental health services in Trieste and other cities of the region. In 2000, she joined the World Health Organization (WHO) in Kosovo as a mental health officer. In 2001, she moved to Albania, holding the same position until 2006, when she was appointed WHO Representative to Albania. In both countries, she worked closely with the Ministries of Health to help establish comprehensive community-based mental health systems. In 2007, Mrs. Kestel joined PAHO as a subregional mental health adviser for the English-speaking Caribbean countries, based in Barbados. Since November 2011, Mrs. Kestel has served as the regional mental health adviser, based in Washington, DC, providing technical cooperation in the mental health field to the region, with special attention to the Caribbean subregion.

Ray Kotwicki, M.D., M.P.H., is passionate about linking excellent clinical care with medical student education. As the director of medical student education for the Department of Psychiatry and Behavioral Sciences at Emory University's School of Medicine, he focuses on helping trainees cultivate not only proficiency in delivery of mental health and primary care medical services, but also medical professionalism. In partnership with Dr. Lisa Bernstein from the Department of Internal Medicine, Dr. Kotwicki co-directs the Emory School of Medicine's "Becoming A Doctor" curriculum, a 4-year longitudinal program designed to train medical students in the highest standards of clinical skills, professionalism, ethics, and medical professionals' roles and responsibilities within society. He received the prestigious Dean's Golden Apple Teaching Award in 2010. In addition to his responsibilities in education, Dr. Kotwicki serves as chief medical officer of Skyland Trail, a private nonprofit community treatment facility recently awarded the American Psychiatric Association's Gold Award. Skyland Trail's mission is to inspire people with mental illness to thrive through a holistic program of evidence-based psychiatric treatment, integrated medical care, research, and education. Services offered at Skyland Trail include residential treatment, partial hospitalization, intensive outpatient care, and community-based health navigation support, based on patients' individualized recovery plan and needs. Emory's medical students beginning their psychiatry clerkships orient at Skyland Trail, and several remain at the program for the duration of their mental health training. Dr. Kotwicki is past president of the Board of Positive Impact, Inc., a prevention and service delivery program for people infected with or affected by HIV/AIDS, and currently sits on the Board of Directors for Georgia Psychiatric Physicians Association and Mental Health America of Georgia. He contributes to the Emory community in other ways as well, including roles within the Medical School's Admission Committee, Progress and Promotions Committee, and Executive Curriculum Committee. The National Alliance on Mental Illness honored Dr. Kotwicki's many contributions to training law enforcement officers on crisis intervention techniques by naming him an "Exemplary Psychiatrist in Georgia" in 2007.

Ronaldo Laranjeira, Ph.D., is a professor of psychiatry and addictive behaviors at the Federal University of São Paulo, and the director of the National

Institute of Alcohol and Drugs Policies, Brazil. He finished his Ph.D. at the London University, National Addiction Center, with Professor Griffith Edwards in 1995. He returned to São Paulo, Brazil, and set up an Addiction Research Unit. His work at the National Addiction center has focused on several areas: organizing for the first time in Brazil two national household surveys on alcohol and drugs, in collaboration with Dr. Raul Caetano from Texas University; working on the study and implementation of alcohol and drug policies in the community, such as the closing of bars in the city of Diadema, zero blood alcohol concentration for drivers, partner violence related to alcohol, and violence and mortality related to "crack/cocaine" use; implementing an alcohol and drug treatment system in the State of São Paulo. Dr. Laranjeira is also a member of the Department of Addiction of the Brazilian Psychiatric Association.

Kenneth Leonard, Ph.D., is the director of the Research Institute on Addictions and a research professor of psychiatry at the University at Buffalo Medical School. He received his Ph.D. in clinical psychology from Kent State University in 1981, and postdoctoral training in psychiatric and alcohol epidemiology at the Western Psychiatric Institute and the Clinic at the University of Pittsburgh. He is a Fellow in Divisions 50 (Addictions) and 28 (Psychopharmacology and Substance Abuse) in the American Psychological Association, and is a former president of Division 50. He is a member of the International Society for Research on Aggression, and is currently a council member for this organization. He is also a member of the Research Society on Alcoholism. He has been a member of the editorial board of the *Journal of Studies on Alcohol* since 1992, a member of the Board of Directors of Alcoholism: Clinical and Experimental Research, and a member of the Editorial Advisory Board, Review of Aggression and Violent Behavior. He served as associate editor for the *Journal of Abnormal Psychology* and has been consulting editor for the *Journal of Abnormal Psychology* and for *Psychological Bulletin*. Dr. Leonard's research interests have centered on the interpersonal and familial influences on substance abuse, as well as the influence of substance abuse on interpersonal and family processes. He is internationally recognized for his research on substance abuse and intimate partner violence, but has been concerned with the impact of alcoholism on child development and the role of marital and family processes in the prevention and treatment of substance abuse. He has also conducted research focused on the prevalence of violence in the lives of young men and women, and factors associated with "bar room" violence.

Michael Luo has worked at *The New York Times* since 2003. He became deputy metropolitan editor in 2014, helping to oversee coverage of New York City and the surrounding region and directing a team of reporters focusing on investigations and long-form feature projects. Before becoming an editor, he was a reporter for 3 years in *The New York Times*'s investigations cluster. Much of his work explored gaps in gun laws and their impact on public safety, as well as the influence of the gun lobby. He spent 2012 working on investigative stories related to the presidential campaign. Mr. Luo has written about economics and the recession as a national correspondent; covered the 2008 presidential campaign and the 2010 midterm elections; and done stints in the Washington, DC, and Baghdad bureaus. He started at the paper on the metropolitan desk. Before joining *The New York Times*, he was a national writer at The Associated Press, where he wrote narrative feature stories from around the country. He has also worked at *Newsday* and the *Los Angeles Times*. In 2002, he won a George Polk Award for criminal justice reporting and a Livingston Award for Young Journalists for a series of articles on three poor, mentally retarded African Americans in Alabama who were in prison for killing a baby who probably never existed. As a result of the series, two of the prisoners were freed; the third remained in prison on a separate charge. Mr. Luo graduated in 1998 from Harvard University, where he majored in government.

Vickie M. Mays, Ph.D., M.S.P.H., is a professor in the Department of Psychology in the College of Letters and Sciences, as well as a professor in the Department of Health Policy and Management. Professor Mays is also the director of the University of California, Los Angeles, Center on Research, Education, Training, and Strategic Communication on Minority Health Disparities. She teaches courses on health status and health behaviors of racial and ethnic minority groups, research ethics in biomedical and behavioral research in racial/ethnic minority populations, research methods in minority research, as well as courses on social determinants of mental disorders and psychopathology. She holds a Ph.D. in clinical psychology and an M.S.P.H. in health services, with postdoctoral training in psychiatric epidemiology, survey research as it applies to ethnic minorities (University of Michigan) and health policy (RAND). Professor Mays' research primarily focuses on the mental and physical health disparities affecting racial and ethnic minority populations. She has a long history of research and policy development in the area of contextual factors that surround HIV/AIDS in racial and ethnic minorities. This work ranges from looking at barriers to education and services to understanding racial-based immunological differences that may contribute to health outcome disparities. Other areas of research include looking at the role of perceived and actual discrimination on mental and physical health outcomes, particularly as these factors impact downstream disease outcomes. Her mental health research examines availability, access, and quality of mental health services for racial, ethnic, and sexual minorities. She is the co-principal investigator of the California

Quality of Life Survey, a population-based study of more than 2,200 Californians on the prevalence of mental health disorders and the contextual factors associated with those disorders.

James A. Mercy, Ph.D., is a special adviser for strategic directions at the Division of Violence Prevention in the National Center for Injury Prevention and Control of the Centers for Disease Control and Prevention (CDC). He began working at CDC in a newly formed activity to examine violence as a public health problem and, over the past two decades, has helped to develop the public health approach to violence and has conducted and overseen numerous studies of the epidemiology of youth suicide, family violence, homicide, and firearm injuries. Dr. Mercy also served as a co-editor of the *World Report on Violence and Health* prepared by the World Health Organization (WHO) and served on the editorial board of the United Nation's Secretary General's Study of Violence Against Children. Most recently he has been working on a global partnership with UNICEF, the President's Emergency Plan for AIDS Relief, WHO, and others to end sexual violence against girls. His recent publications include "Attention-Deficit/Hyperactivity Disorder, Conduct Disorder, and Young Adult Intimate Partner Violence" (*Archives of General Psychiatry*, 2010) and "Sexual Violence and Its Health Consequences for Female Children in Swaziland: A Cluster Survey Study" (*Lancet*, 2009).

Klaus A. Miczek, Ph.D., is the Moses Hunt Professor of Psychology, Psychiatry, Pharmacology, and Neuroscience at Tufts University. He has served on research review committees for the National Institute on Drug Abuse, National Institute of Mental Health, National Institute on Alcoholism and Alcohol Abuse (NIAAA), and National Center for Research Resources. He was a member of the National Academy of Sciences panel on "Understanding and Preventing Violence" (1989–1992), as well as its ILAR/NRC panel on the "Psychological Well-Being of Primates." He has been the coordinating and principal editor of *Psychopharmacology* since 1992, and he serves on the editorial board of half a dozen other journals in this area. He was the president of the Division of Psychopharmacology, and of the Behavioral Pharmacology Society, and chaired the Committee on Animals in Research and Ethics of the American Psychology Association. He has received numerous prizes including the Solvay Duphar Award of the Division of Psychopharmacology and Substance Abuse of the American Psychological Association, a MERIT award from NIAAA, and Silver Medals of the Charles University (Czech Republic). In 1997, the president of the Federal Republic of Germany bestowed the Knight's Cross of the Order of Merit on him. Dr. Miczek was named the Boerhaave professor at the medical faculty of Leiden University (Netherlands) and was a two-time Japan

International Science and Technology Fellow at the University of Tokyo. He was visiting professor at La Sapienza University in Rome, the Charles University in Prague, and at the University of Tuebingen in Germany. In 2006, Tufts University recognized Dr. Miczek with the Distinguished Scholar Award, and he was elected fellow in the American Association for the Advancement of Science. He published some 200 research journal articles and 40 reviews, and edited 20 volumes on psychopharmacological research concerning brain mechanisms of aggression, anxiety, social stress, and abuse of alcohol and other drugs. He was originally educated in Berlin (Germany) and received his Ph.D. in biopsychology from the University of Chicago. Currently, the work in Dr. Miczek's laboratory investigates two problems in the areas of (1) stress and drug abuse, and (2) behavioral neurobiology of aggression. First, members of the laboratory aim to learn about neuroadaptive mechanisms via which specific social stressors can intensify compulsive drug use or alternatively engender depressive-like anhedonia. Second, they are seeking to characterize the neurobiological features of those individuals who engage in escalated aggression after alcohol consumption.

Margaret M. Murray, Ph.D., M.S.W., is the director of the Global Alcohol Research Program, National Institute on Alcohol Abuse and Alcoholism (NIAAA), National Institutes of Health. Dr. Murray directs NIAAA's efforts in international research collaboration spanning each of the Institute's priorities in biomedical, epidemiological, prevention, and treatment research. This includes serving on U.S. Science and Technology Committees, NIH, and government-wide initiatives in global health, and representing NIAAA to multilateral organizations such as WHO. She is primarily responsible for facilitating collaborative relationships at the individual institute and scientist level. Dr. Murray is also a lecturer at the National Catholic School of Social Service at Catholic University, where she teaches the foundation courses in social welfare policy in the master of social work program.

Toben Nelson, Sc.D., is a primary faculty member of the Alcohol Epidemiology Program at the University of Minnesota School of Public Health. He has research interests in health policy, organizational change, health behavior during developmental transitions, social determinants of health, program evaluation, prevention of alcohol-attributable harm, violence prevention, and motor vehicle safety.

Dustin Pardini, Ph.D., conducts research that involves elucidating the precursors and outcomes associated with the development of antisocial behavior (e.g., violence, theft) from childhood to adulthood, as well as evaluating the impact that early psychosocial interventions can have on these problems. Much of this work has focused on the development and treatment of conduct problems among youth exhibiting callous and unemotional (CU) traits. Over the past 8 years, this has involved analyzing data from two of the most extensive longitudinal studies ever conducted within the United States: the Pittsburgh Youth Study (co-director) and the Pittsburgh Girls Study. Dr. Pardini's innovative research directly influences the adoption of the new conduct disorder specifier based on the presence of CU traits (called limited prosocial emotions) in the *Diagnostic and Statistical Manual, Fifth Edition* (DSM-5), and earned him the Early Career Contribution Award from the Society of the Scientific Study of Psychopathy (2013). He is currently serving as a consultant to members of the Conduct Disorders Research Committee for the eleventh revision of the *International Classification of Diseases* (ICD-11). He has also been involved in research designed to evaluate the effectiveness of interventions for children exhibiting early aggression, including the Stop Now and Plan (SNAP) and the Resources to Enhance the Adjustment of Children (REACH) programs.

Michael Phillips, M.D., M.P.H., is currently the director of the Suicide Research and Prevention Center of the Shanghai Mental Health Center, executive director of the WHO Collaborating Center for Research and Training in Suicide Prevention at Beijing Hui Long Guan Hospital, professor of psychiatry and global health at Emory University, professor of clinical psychiatry and clinical epidemiology at Columbia University, vice chairperson of the Chinese Society for Injury Prevention and Control, and treasurer of the International Association for Suicide Prevention. He is currently the principal investigator on a number of multicenter collaborative projects on suicide, depression, and schizophrenia. His recent publications include "Repetition of Suicide Attempts: Data from Emergency Care Settings in Five Culturally Different Low- and Middle-Income Countries Participating in the WHO SUPRE-MISS Study" (*Crisis*, 2010) and "Nonfatal Suicidal Behavior Among Chinese Women Who Have Been Physically Abused by Their Male Intimate Partners" (*Suicide and Life-Threatening Behavior*, 2009). Dr. Phillips is a Canadian citizen who has been a permanent resident of China for more than 25 years. He runs a number of research training courses each year; supervises Chinese and foreign graduate students; helps coordinate WHO mental health activities in China; promotes increased awareness of the importance of addressing China's huge suicide problem; and advocates improving the quality, comprehensiveness, and access to mental health services around the country.

Mark L. Rosenberg, M.D., M.P.P., is the executive director of the Task Force for Global Health. Previously, for 20 years, Dr. Rosenberg was at the Centers for Disease Control and Prevention (CDC), where he led its work in violence prevention and later became the first permanent director of the National Center for Injury Prevention and Control. He also held the position of special assistant for behavioral science in the Office of the Deputy Director (HIV/AIDS). Dr. Rosenberg is board certified in both psychiatry and internal medicine with training in public policy. He is on the faculty at Morehouse Medical School, Emory Medical School, and the Rollins School of Public Health at Emory University. Dr. Rosenberg's research and programmatic interests are concentrated on injury control and violence prevention, HIV/AIDS, and child well-being, with special attention to behavioral sciences, evaluation, and health communications. He has authored more than 120 publications and recently co-authored the book *Real Collaboration: What It Takes for Global Health to Succeed* (University of California Press, 2010). Dr. Rosenberg has received numerous awards including the Surgeon General's Exemplary Service Medal. He is a member of the National Academy of Medicine. Dr. Rosenberg's organization, the Task Force for Global Health, participated in the National Academies of Sciences, Engineering, and Medicine–sponsored workshop Violence Prevention in Low- and Middle-Income Countries: Finding a Place on the Global Agenda, and the Task Force remains interested in helping to continue the momentum of the workshop through the Forum on Global Violence Prevention. The Task Force is heavily involved in the delivery of a number of global health programs and sees many ways in which interpersonal violence and conflict exacerbate serious health problems and inequities.

Harvey Rosenthal has more than 38 years of experience working to promote public mental health services and policies that advance the recovery, rehabilitation, rights, and community inclusion of people with psychiatric disabilities. Since 1993, Mr. Rosenthal has served as the executive director of the New York Association of Psychiatric Rehabilitation Services (NYAPRS), a peer-led consumer-provider partnership that has worked to improve services, social conditions, and public policies in New York and nationally that touch the lives of people with psychiatric disabilities. Under his leadership, NYAPRS has supported a strong grassroots advocacy community, developed recovery training programs for community providers, and has created nationally replicated peer-service and economic development innovations. Mr. Rosenthal is currently providing a broad array of training and technical assistance nationally to promote peer-run and recovery services. He regularly works to fight stigma, discrimination, and coercion and to expand informed choice protections. Mr. Rosenthal currently serves on the board of the Bazelon Center for Mental Health Law, acts as co-chair of the Peer Leaders Interest Group for ACMHA: the College for Behavioral Health Leadership, and is a member of the consumer-survivor subcommittee to the Center Mental Health Services

Advisory Group. He is a member of New York's Medicaid Redesign Team and its Most Integrated Settings Coordinating Council. His interest in promoting mental health recovery is also personal, dating back to his own hospitalization at age 19.

Elyn R. Saks, Ph.D., J.D., specializes in mental health law, criminal law, and children and the law. Her recent research focused on ethical dimensions of psychiatric research and forced treatment of the mentally ill. She teaches Mental Health Law, Mental Health Law and the Criminal Justice System, and Advanced Family Law: The Rights and Interests of Children. She served as the University of Southern California (USC) Law's associate dean for research from 2005 to 2010 and also teaches at the Institute of Psychiatry and the Law at the Keck School of Medicine at USC and is an adjunct professor of psychiatry at the University of California, San Diego. Professor Saks was a 2009 recipient of a MacArthur Foundation fellowship and in fall 2010 announced she is using funds from the "Genius Grant" to create the Saks Institute for Mental Health Law, Policy, and Ethics. The Institute spotlights one important mental health issue per academic year and is a collaborative effort that includes faculty from seven USC departments: law, psychiatry, psychology, social work, gerontology, philosophy, and engineering. Professor Saks recently published *The Center Cannot Hold: My Journey Through Madness* (Hyperion, 2007), a memoir about her struggles and successes with schizophrenia and acute psychosis. Other publications include *Refusing Care: Forced Treatment and the Rights of the Mentally Ill* (University of Chicago Press, 2002), *Interpreting Interpretation: The Limits of Hermeneutic Psychoanalysis* (Yale University Press, 1999), and *Jekyll on Trial: Multiple Personality Disorder and Criminal Law* (with Stephen H. Behnke, New York University Press, 1997). Before joining the USC Law faculty in 1989, Professor Saks was an attorney in Connecticut and an instructor at the University of Bridgeport School of Law. She graduated summa cum laude from Vanderbilt University before earning her master of letters from Oxford University and her J.D. from Yale Law School, where she also edited the *Yale Law Journal*. She holds a Ph.D. in psychoanalytic science from the New Center for Psychoanalysis. Professor Saks is a member of Phi Beta Kappa; an affiliate member of the American Psychoanalytic Association; a board member of Mental Health Advocacy Services; and a member of the Los Angeles Psychoanalytic Foundation, Robert J. Stoller Foundation, and American Law Institute. Professor Saks won both the Associate's Award for Creativity in Research and Scholarship and the Phi Kappa Phi Faculty Recognition Award in 2004.

Kimberly A. Scott, M.S.P.H., has been a senior program officer on the Health and Medicine Division's Board on Global Health since September

2005. She currently directs two forums: one on Global Violence Prevention and the other on Public–Private Partnerships for Global Health and Safety. She is also co-directing a workshop on Evaluation Methods for Large-Scale, Complex, Multinational Global Health Initiatives. From 2009 to 2013, she was the study co-director for the outcome and impact evaluation of the U.S. global HIV/AIDS initiative (i.e., the President's Emergency Plan for AIDS Relief, or PEPFAR). Her portfolio of work for the National Academies also includes a mix of consensus studies, workshops, and other activities, including the Evaluation of the Implementation of PEPFAR; Preventing Violence in Low- and Middle-Income Countries; the Assessment of the Role of Intermittent Preventive Treatment for Malaria in Infants; Depression, Parenting Practices, and the Health Development of Children; and Achieving Global Sustainable Surveillance for Zoonotic Diseases. Before joining the National Academies, she was an analyst on the health care team at the U.S. Government Accountability Office. Before returning to graduate school, she coordinated a foundation-funded program at Duke University's Center for Health Policy, Law, and Management to integrate public and private mental health services with the continuum of care for people living with and affected by HIV/AIDS in 54 counties in North Carolina. For 6 years, she served as the executive director of a Ryan White–funded HIV/AIDS consortium, developing a comprehensive ambulatory care system for 21 mostly rural counties in North Carolina. Previous North Carolina health-related committee service includes several advisory committees to the governor of North Carolina and to the secretary of the North Carolina Department of Health and Human Services for programmatic and policy issues related to HIV care, prevention, and treatment, as well as substance abuse prevention and treatment. She received an M.S.P.H. in health policy analysis from the University of North Carolina, Chapel Hill. As an Echols Scholar, she completed her undergraduate studies at the University of Virginia.

Sharon Stephan, Ph.D., is a leading figure in advancing school mental health (SMH) research, training, policy, and practice at national, state, and local levels. Dr. Stephan is a licensed clinical psychologist and a tenured associate professor at the University of Maryland School of Medicine, Division of Child and Adolescent Psychiatry. After providing direct mental health promotion and treatment service for several years in the Baltimore City Public Schools, Dr. Stephan was appointed as director of research for the national Center for School Mental Health (CSMH) in 2002. From 2005 to 2010, she guided the advancement of research and policy in her role as the CSMH director of research and analysis, and in 2010 became the CSMH principal investigator and co-director with Dr. Nancy Lever. Dr. Stephan has extensive expertise and leadership related to implementation science, quality assessment and improvement, evaluation and outcome measurement, and SMH service delivery, workforce development, and state and local capacity building. Her evaluation and project direction experience is extensive, having served as the principal investigator, site principal investigator, or lead evaluator for several projects including two SAMHSA Systems of Care evaluations; the SAMHSA Healthy Transitions Initiative evaluation; two R01s from NIMH on Enhancing SMH Quality; Maryland's Early Childhood Mental Health Consultation Evaluation; the National Assembly on School-Based Health Care (NASBHC) Mental Health Education and Training Initiative; Youth Moving Others Through Voices of Experience; Maryland's Governor's Office for Children Evidence-Based Practices Fidelity and Outcomes Evaluation; and the Baltimore SMH Initiative. Dr. Stephan has published extensively, with many peer-reviewed articles and editorial service, and is a highly regarded and sought after speaker and trainer. She has held leadership roles on several national committees, including the SAMHSA Federal-National partnership, the National Evidence-Based Practice Consortium, the National Coordinating Committee on School Health and Safety (NCCSHS), the CDC SMH Capacity Building Project, the National Assembly on School-Based Health Care (Evaluation and Quality Panel, Training and Technical Assistance Panel), and the SAMHSA National Child Traumatic Stress Network Trauma Services Adaptation Center for Schools (School Treatment Workgroup and Military Families Workgroup).

Daniel W. Webster, Sc.D., M.P.H., is a professor of health policy and management and directs the Ph.D. program in Health and Public Policy at the Johns Hopkins Bloomberg School of Public Health. Dr. Webster is director of the Johns Hopkins Center for Gun Policy and Research, deputy director for research for the Johns Hopkins Center for the Prevention of Youth Violence, and core faculty of the Johns Hopkins Center for Injury Research and Policy. Dr. Webster holds a joint appointment as professor in the School of Education's Division of Public Safety Leadership at Johns Hopkins, and is a senior research fellow with the Police Executive Research Forum. Dr. Webster is one of the nation's leading experts on firearm policy and the prevention of gun violence. He is co-editor of *Reducing Gun Violence in America: Informing Policy with Evidence and Analysis* (Johns Hopkins University Press, 2013). He has published numerous articles on firearm policy, youth gun acquisition and carrying, the prevention of gun violence, intimate partner violence, and adolescent violence prevention. He has studied the effects of several violence prevention interventions, including state firearm and alcohol policies, policing strategies, street outreach and conflict mediation, public education campaigns, and school-based curricula. Dr. Webster teaches Understanding and Preventing Violence, Research and

Evaluation Methods for Health Policy, and graduate seminar in health and public policy.

David B. Wexler, Ph.D., is a professor of law and director of the International Network on Therapeutic Jurisprudence at the University of Puerto Rico in San Juan, Puerto Rico, and Distinguished Research Professor of Law, Rogers College of Law, Tucson, Arizona. He received the American Psychiatric Association's Manfred S. Guttmacher Forensic Psychiatry Award; chaired the American Bar Association's Commission on Mental Disability and the Law; chaired the Association of American Law Schools' Section on Law and Mental Disability; chaired the Advisory Board of the National Center for State Courts' Institute on Mental Disability and Law; was a member of the Panel on Legal Issues of the President's Commission on Mental Health; was a member of the National Commission on the Insanity Defense; served as vice president of the International Academy of Law and Mental Health; received the New York University School of Law Distinguished Alumnus Legal Scholarship/Teaching Award; received the Distinguished Service Award from the National Center for State Courts; and served as a member of the MacArthur Foundation Research Network on Mental Health and the Law. Dr. Wexler has been named an Honorary Distinguished Member of the American Psychology-Law Society. In October 2012, at its Congress in Pontevedra, Galicia, Spain, Dr. Wexler was named Honorary President of the Iberoamerican Association of Therapeutic Jurisprudence, an organization headquartered at the University of Vigo. Therapeutic jurisprudence writing is now in 10 languages, and some of Dr. Wexler's own work has been translated to Hebrew, Portuguese, Spanish, and Urdu. He is a consultant on therapeutic jurisprudence to the National Judicial Institute of Canada and the Judicial Academy of Puerto Rico, and has served as a Fulbright Senior Specialist, lecturing on therapeutic jurisprudence in Australia and New Zealand. Before entering law teaching, Dr. Wexler practiced for the Criminal Division of the U.S. Department of Justice. He first explicated the therapeutic jurisprudence perspective in a paper written in 1987. He and Professor Bruce Winick of the University of Miami worked together to further develop the area, which is now of interest to practitioners and academics of many disciplines and nations.

Dieter Wolke, Ph.D., studied at the University of Kiel in Germany and obtained his Ph.D. from the University of London Faculty of Science. He has worked at different colleges of the University of London (i.e., Institute of Education; King's College; and the Institute of Child Health, Hospital for Sick Children) and the Universities of Munich, Hertfordshire (chair), Bristol (chair in lifespan psychology, and deputy director of the Avon Longitudinal Study [ALSPAC]), and was guest professor of the University of Zurich and scientific director of the Jacobs Foundation, Zurich (2004–2006) before joining the University of Warwick. Dr. Wolke is currently professor of developmental psychology and individual differences in the Department of Psychology (Faculty of Science) and in the Division of Mental Health and Well-being (Warwick Medical School) at the University of Warwick. He is the lead of the Lifespan Health and Well-being Research Stream in the Department of Psychology. Much of his research is interdisciplinary (psychology, social, and medical sciences), longitudinal, and in the field of developmental psychopathology. His major research topics are (1) peer or sibling victimization (bullying): precursors, consequences, and interventions; (2) early regulatory problems in infancy and their long-term consequences; (3) how preterm birth affects brain development, psychological development, and quality of life. He is involved as principal investigator/co-principal investigator in a range of follow-up studies in the United Kingdom and Germany, including the ALSPAC cohort, EPICure Study, the Bavarian Longitudinal Study, and the U.K. Household Longitudinal Study (Understanding Society), which is the largest longitudinal panel study in the world, including more than 100,000 people with a special interest in biomarkers. Dr. Wolke has published more than 200 articles in leading journals and is on the editorial boards of several journals and several scientific advisory boards.